DONALD BARTHELME
POSTMODERNIST AMERICAN WRITER

DONALD BARTHELME
POSTMODERNIST AMERICAN WRITER

Michael Thomas Hudgens

Studies in American Literature
Volume 43

The Edwin Mellen Press
Lewiston•Queenston•Lampeter

Library of Congress Cataloging-in-Publication Data

Hudgens, Michael Thomas.
  Donald Barthelme, postmodernist American writer / Michael Thomas Hudgens.
    p. cm. -- (Studies in American literature ; v. 43)
  Includes bibliographical references and index.
  ISBN 0-7734-7479-X
    1. Barthelme, Donald--Criticism and interpretation. 2. Experimental fiction,
American--History and criticism. 3. Postmodernism (Literature)--United States. I. Title.
II. Studies in American literature (Lewiston, N.Y.) ; v. 43.

  PS3552.A76 Z694 2001
  813'.54--dc21

                                                                    2001032950

This is volume 43 in the continuing series
Studies in American Literature
Volume 43 ISBN 0-7734-7479-X
SAL Series ISBN 0-88946-166-X

A CIP catalog record for this book is available from the British Library.

          The Edwin Mellen Press   The Edwin Mellen Press
               Box 450   Box 67
          Lewiston, New York   Queenston, Ontario
          USA 14092-0450   CANADA L0S 1L0

                    The Edwin Mellen Press, Ltd.
                    Lampeter, Ceredigion, Wales
                    UNITED KINGDOM SA48 8LT

                 Printed in the United States of America

To Alexander Craig Hudgens

TABLE OF CONTENTS

The story "On Angels" initially appears to be a medley of glittering, accidental material but coheres over the course of 14 paragraphs into a meditation on the loss of centrality in contemporary consciousness. The story is a microcosm of Barthelme's creative dilemma as a Postmodern fiction writer, and involves a major theme in his fiction and a key point in the secondary thesis of the study.

Wilde argues that Barthelme is not a realist, but he himself insists that he is, that his fiction "is a way of dealing with reality." He has positioned himself, Gass says, "in the center of modern consciousness," using everyday materials "to make a treasure out of trash, to see *out* from inside it, the world as it's faceted by colored jewelglass." Barthelme says Joyce did this "in various ways" and sees *Finnegans Wake* as collage. One aim of the study is to show that Barthelme has roots in a key pattern of Joyce's modernism but is able to bring it forward in a contemporary context.

The great Modernist story "The Dead" has parallels to Barthelme's novel *Paradise* and his final short story "Tickets." Several passages of *Finnegans Wake* are analyzed here to illustrate what he calls the effort of the artist to distance himself from the commonplace and to "attain a fresh mode of cognition."

Barthelme's first novel is examined to show him forging fictional values, and acknowledging influences from architecture and painting. Later, though, the novel became a burden for him, "not one of my favorites," he said in several published interviews.

PREFACE

In reading Michael Hudgens' engaging study of the fictional canon of Donald Barthelme, I am reminded of Samuel Taylor Coleridge's injunction on the necessity of a willful suspension of disbelief as a crucial prerequisite for the reading of literature. But I am not reminded of Coleridge in the sense that his injunction is something that Dr. Hudgens needed to entertain in articulating the meaning and acknowledging the magic of Donald Barthelme's contribution to Postmodern American fiction. What strikes me most about the study is that Dr. Hudgens has not had to suspend anything in connecting with Barthelme's postmodern vision or with the artistic means through which that vision was formed and realized. Choose any chapter of this creatively organized study, and you will find that the arguments and evidence brought together within it rest on Dr. Hudgens' intuitive grasp of Barthelme's aesthetics and of his highly individualized quest for the narrative designs with which to reflect that vision. Hudgens understands that this is a fiction writer in whose work the aesthetics of fragmentation are perfectly codified through the unconventional materials Barthelme weaves together to create the semantic mesh of his stories and novels. The resulting voice-driven montages make perfect sense to Hudgens because he is so keenly aware of Barthelme's philosophical orientation and of the absurd cultural ecology informing Barthelme's artistic mandates as a late 20th century fiction writer. He reads Barthelme on Barthelme's own terms, allows him the freedom of his personal definitions of narrative art and his stubborn convictions about his own brand of realism. Hudgens also sees the affinities between Barthelme's self-styled fiction and the experimental urges of other postmodernists such as Coover, Elkin, Gaddis, Gass, Hawkes, Pynchon, and Vonnegut. Thus, the study becomes a montage of its own in framing Barthelme's fiction through lateral glances at Barthelme's contemporaries, and not just in fiction but in painting and architecture as well. Further, the evolution of the discussion even digresses in Barthelme fashion into a portrait of James Joyce and Donald Barthelme as modern and postmodern father and son.

Unlike many of Barthelme's interpreters, then, Hudgens identifies unconditionally with Barthelme's risky quest to create a fictional universe based on contemplation and channeled through the mood swings and associative impulses of the speaking voice. The profiling of that long, painful struggle to "speak the unspeakable" and to amplify the speaking with the shards and detritus of apparently discordant images is Hudgens' main concern and the unifying instrument of his exegesis. Being a reader not needing to suspend his disbelief, he is able to illuminate Barthelme's fiction with the same intuitive leaps of faith that Barthelme used in constructing such a uniquely shaped body of work.

Brian Bedard
University of South Dakota
September 2000

FOREWORD

This study is written in appreciation of and as a way to clarify and interpret the literary function and value of certain artistic choices made by American Postmodernist writer Donald Barthelme as he constructed a fictive realm found in four novels and more than 100 short stories. His choices in designing this work were often made randomly, intuitively, impulsively—and painterly, in the way he pulled apparently accidental material into it. Some of the fiction was shaped by external events and people in his life. In brief, he was less methodical than erratic, but less erratic than double-minded.

Although many of his choices cannot be explained in terms of conventional literary logic, they are no more or no less logical than those of other Postmodern fiction writers, many of whom seek personal salvation and cultural revelation through the contortions of narrative experiment. Barthelme's seemingly arbitrary approach to story focus and content, which I will argue is anything but arbitrary and which in fact operates according to its own painful logic, is the basis for my explication of his fiction in this study. The coherence he achieves through the ingenious manipulation and fusion of seemingly bizarre and disparate narrative elements will be revealed in the course of my discussion and will demonstrate that Barthelme is a successful and significant experimentalist whose work is an underrated and often misperceived artifact of late 20th-century American literature. The canon of his work is an invaluable repository of the literary, philosophical, political, and cultural ecology of his time, but most important is the shaping of it by his distinct and daring sensibility and voice and by his quest for a literature capable of speaking from the center of its own contemporary consciousness to anyone willing to listen closely. What we can gain from listening to Barthelme is what we gain from listening to and spending time with the narrator of Ralph Ellison's *Invisible Man,* who, in concluding that novel, says to the reader, "Who knows but that, on the lower frequencies, I speak for you?"

Commentary on Barthelme was not extensive at this writing. Stanley Trachtenberg's *Understanding Donald Barthelme* contains helpful information on Barthelme's work and details of his career, especially during the 1970s, and tends toward a traditional treatment, as seen in this explanation: "Barthelme frustrates conventional structural expectations by blurring or exchanging the positions held by antagonists in a conflict, indefinitely postponing a climax, or even by substituting the movement of linguistic elements for that of the characters whose lives they describe" (7). Comparable investment in technique, of course, can be found in the fiction of Joyce, Woolf and other Modernists.

Barbara L. Roe's *Donald Barthelme: A Study of the Short Fiction* (Twayne, 1992) complements Trachtenberg: Included are excerpts from her 1988 interview with Barthelme and four of her essays on his work, all of which shed light on the last years his life. Jerome Klinkowitz's 1974 interview with Barthelme, found in *The New Fiction: Interviews with Innovative American Writers,* is highly illuminating. So are three other interviews—by J. D. O'Hara (1981), and Larry McCaffery and Jo Brans (both 1982)—used extensively in this study.

I've also reviewed other helpful articles by Robert Con Davis, Mary Robertson, Richard Walsh, Patrick O'Donnell, Alan Wilde, and Richard Patteson from the 1992 anthology *Critical Essays on Donald Barthelme.* Wilde's piece, "Barthelme Unfair to Kierkegaard," was published in the 1981 *Horizons of Assent: Modernism, Postmodernism, and the Ironic Imagination.* It examines irony in Barthelme's work, while arguing that what appears to be satire offers a vision of the contemporary world. This idea is taken further in "Barthelme in his garden," published in the 1987 *Middle Grounds: Studies in Contemporary American Fiction,* with Wilde asserting that Barthelme shows concern for the state of society. Wilde says, "[M]any of his best stories, not to mention *The Dead Father,* are, whatever their playfulness, nothing if not moral: studies in smallness and risk that endorse an ethic of tentative, provisional pleasures against a background of daily life that frequently remains as frustrating as it is drab" (165)

Additional insights into Barthelme's artistic choices are revealed in critical commentary by Postmodernists William Gass and John Barth. In the 1970 *Fiction and the Figures of Life,* Gass explains in "The Leading Edge of the Trash Phenomenon" how Barthelme makes use of cultural trash, leveling it into "a single plane of truth, of relevance, of style, of value—a flatland junkyard" (101)

Barth's eulogy to Barthelme, "Thinking Man's Minimalist: Honoring Barthelme," published in the 3 September 1989 *New York Times Book Review,* discusses materials in the novel *Snow White* and "those often plotless marvels of which he published some seven volumes over 20 years, from *Come Back, Dr. Caligari* in 1964 to *Overnight to Many Distant Cities* in 1983" (9). He praises Barthelme's "urbane and urban semi-Surrealism" and places him in the ranks of "post-contemporaries" Robert Coover, Stanley Elkin, William Gaddis, William Gass, John Hawkes, Thomas Pynchon and Kurt Vonnegut (9). In Barth's *The Friday Book: Essays and Other Nonfiction,* 1984, and in *Further Fridays: Essays, Lectures, and Other Nonfiction, 1984–94,* he tries to trace the serpentine path of literary Postmodernism, ending up with this comprehensive statement: "[T]he Postmodernist novel has been influenced more by the example of Gabriel García Márquez than he has been influenced by Postmodernist literary theory. . . . The individual terrific writer, the individual terrific work, is the main thing" (*Further Fridays* 310).

Finally, a 1991 George Washington University Ph.D. dissertation "Donald Barthelme: The Modernist Underpinnings of a Post-Modernist Fiction" by Gary

P. Walton is commendable for its treatment of Joyce as a way to understand Barthelme. Walton argues that Barthelme owes much to the Modernists, especially Joyce, since both created constructed objects, "self-consciously aware of their own dynamics." Walton devotes a chapter to an analysis of *Ulysses*. The inclusion of *Finnegans Wake* in my study was prompted by Walton's work and Umberto Eco's statement in his *Postscript to The Name of the Rose*, 1984:

> Look at Joyce. The *Portrait* is the story of an attempt at the Modern. *Dubliners,* even if it comes before, is more modern than *Portrait. Ulysses* is on the borderline. *Finnegans Wake* is already postmodern, or at least it imitates the postmodern discourses: it demands, in order to be understood, not the negation of the already said, but its ironic rethinking. (68)

This study views Donald Barthelme in his own context—upscale New York City, the art circuit and the *New Yorker,* where he made his reputation and had a relatively loyal readership. He had to take artistic risks while continuing to entertain his audience, and he knew that one failure—his story "Sentence," for example—could diminish his reputation.

Included is analysis of his final short stories and last two novels, *The King* and *Paradise,* with the hope of giving the reader a more precise, revealing, and seemly means of understanding and evaluating Barthelme, both as an individual Postmodernist and a major contributor to Postmodernist fiction. Such an approach I believe to be appropriate because of the disorderly and highly individualistic nature of Postmodernist expression.

Postmodernism, and especially literary Postmodernism, can be many things, depending on the artist. As a concept, it lacks unity—one of the reasons it has never been widely accepted or even understood. Postmodernist expression is generally considered to be a reaction against established forms and cultural perceptions such as the variants of High Modernism appearing in painting, sculpture, architecture, dance, and literature during the last 100 years. For the

Postmodernist response to be effective, the artist must refute each form individually, rather than collectively, but this results in numerous variations, as seen in literary Postmodernism where there is no distinct core. Barth does one thing, Pynchon another. The Postmodernist work seems to be a variation of the form it seeks to refute and replace; it could be viewed as an extension of the original, dependent on it. The result, instead of a break between the two forms, is more a shifting of elements. The Postmodernist work accepts structure but mostly in deconstructed patterns.

Postmodernism also reacts to a changing society and economic order, especially as reflected and shaped in a mass media where confusion reigns, and incoherence and hysteria are the norm. The Postmodernist stance might be that culture, society, and our collective sense of reality are so out of control that the proper response can only be irrational. It's as if the writer were reporting on the Apocalypse from within, proclaiming the horror, however operatically, and then shrugging it off—why make choices, when everything so easily co-exists with its antithesis?—and moving on to survey the next abomination.

An identifiable literary and cultural enemy is often needed for a movement to create worthwhile tension, and for Postmodernists frequently the enemy becomes the plain, old, down-home American tawdriness so evident in popular culture—the trivia of politics, the ostentation of Super Bowls, the voyeurism of talk shows. With artistic shrewdness Postmodernist writers accept and even embrace the reality presented to them. They are drawn to commercial kitsch, and if the traditional boundaries are diminished between high culture and low, between fine art and commercial, all the better because all the more accurate. The wholesome, bland types found in 1950s television sitcoms—or anything else mundane and mindless—can be useful material, not as avenues to Truth but to propose that there are no universal truths. Among the many examples of this are

Kurt Vonnegut's novel *Breakfast of Champions,* Peter Handke's play *Offending the Audience,* and Grace Paley's short story "The Pale Pink Roast."

Postmodernism is not parody. It might mimic the original, but with a neutral representation, without malice aforethought—and without sympathy. Parody, mocking by making use of an original's odd characteristics, assumes that somewhere there exists a linguistic norm, whereas the Postmodernist writer has decided that any such standard has long ceased to exist and has been rendered obsolete by such forces as atomic bombs, sexual freedom, AIDS, political scandals, and crime—all contributing to the trivialization of culture and the resultant deterioration of language and literacy.

Postmodernism imitates but does so without prejudice. A Postmodernist work is never a masque. Instead of being a dissembler, the Postmodernist is more like a primitive shaman, wearing the mask of the original, speaking through it, even using the original's own words, as seen in the novels of Thomas Pynchon, the stories of Robert Coover, certain of Joy Harjo's work—the book she edited with Patricia Blanco, *Reinventing the Enemy's Language*—and Margaret Atwood's story "Happy Endings." An architectural example of this artistic appropriation is Postmodernist Robert Venturi's Guild House, an apartment complex built during the early 1960s in an old section of Philadelphia. By giving this structure the low-cost, dark-red-brick look of the typical urban renewal project, Venturi has managed to make it do more than merely blend with the neighborhood; it *speaks* for the neighborhood and is quite shaman-like in doing so. (One could also argue that it is ultimately refuting the character of the neighborhood by bringing into the light.) Guild House, incidentally, is said by Trachtenberg to be the "clearest visual equivalent" to Barthelme's fiction (19). Wearing such a mask, then, the Postmodernist work can be about itself, about art in general or about the failure of art.

Postmodernist writers, directly or indirectly, often concern themselves with how society has lost its awareness of history and become imprisoned in the present. Barthelme animates this theme deftly in his novel *Paradise*. Whatever the causes for society's isolation from its foundations, the mass media has substituted formulaic, oversimplified pop images as the primary reality. Advertising for consumer products, especially in the form of the music video and institutional spot, employs old video clips featuring deceased celebrities and leaders such as Martin Luther King, Jr., U.S. Presidents, and even the Founding Fathers. This cloning, of course, has its own logic, which is useful to the Postmodernist. In fact, the "reality" presented in Postmodernist work could exist entirely in the medium of television itself with its relentless, indiscriminate, and incoherent procession of images so like the shadows of the exterior world falling across the interior walls of Plato's cave.

All of these processes and points of view are found in Barthelme's work. Why he took the particular artistic path he did in blending them his own way is partially explained in "Not-Knowing," a 1985 speech-essay, with his statement: "[W]e are looking for the as-yet unspeakable, the as-yet unspoken" (117). His path on this quest is a twisted one that sometimes required leaps and bounds that ended—or appeared to—in monumental stumbles. He took heat for his positions and statements, even from a fellow Postmodernist he greatly admired, William Gass, who soundly rebuked him for his pessimism (103). Nevertheless, Barthelme continued to experiment, putting his reputation in peril as he tried both to advance fiction and keep it alive as a cultural compass.

There is no argument that for a majority of readers Barthelme's work appears to suffer from a failure of form. This is a common conclusion reached after a first reading, which is all that some are willing to give. But it must be remembered that early in the twentieth century, many readers were initially put off by *Ulysses*, while others, the doggedly resolute and the merely curious, pushed on, determined to prove their prowess over the puzzle before them.

As the study shows, much of Barthelme's work is accessible, because like Joyce's, the fragments that comprise it are familiar to everyone—recognizable dialogues and monologues of the street and everyday occurrences, however oddly juxtaposed. And from them come the occasional and fabulous Barthelme construction that connects the disparate elements, sometimes through narrative voice alone, and rises or even soars above a barren landscape.

Certain readers, the inquisitive and the determined, are willing to reread, to remain open to narrative experimentation, to individual style, and to irreverent perspectives. This study is aimed at such readers. They might be professionals or students with an interest in Barthelme and in Postmodernist literature—in short, anyone determined, as Barthelme said, referring to literary Postmodernism in general, "to slap a saddle on this rough beast" (115). This statement, as my study will show, can apply to his work too.

Barthelme spent much of his life turning out what Barth has called "self-conscious, process-oriented, and fabulistic writing" (*Further Fridays* 125) Like many living in the Nixon years and in the aftermath, Barthelme expressed anger toward middlebrow American culture in his work, including what several critics believe to be his best novel, *The Dead Father*. Later writing included in the study reveals how he began to mellow during the 1980s, taking a highminded approach in his 1985 story, "Basil from Her Garden," and the following year with *Paradise*, which comes close to the conventional novel. *Paradise* and his final story "Tickets" reveal the shaman unmasked.

In "Not-Knowing," he praises Stéphane Mallarmé for his "acts of poetic intuition" that "point not toward the external world but toward the Absolute" (117). Acts of poetic intuition appear in Barthelme's work too, and in fact "poetic intuition" could function as a password, an open-sesame to some of his seemingly inaccessible narrative. His quest for the objective correlatives of his own time and place is the basis of some of his choices. One day, for example, he might have ventured past a carwash in midtown Manhattan and heard the workers within the structure shouting, "Let's go! Let's go!" It was like an object sticking out of a rubbish bin, and it must have been right—just so—and he took it home with him for later use. The time finally came: it would close his last story.

The study will show modern painting to have been a major force in Barthelme's making the creative narrative choices he did. A favored technique is collage, diverse objects pasted to a canvas for the purpose of being regarded and understood *simultaneously*, like David Bowie in the film *The Man Who Fell to Earth* regarding all 57 television screens at once. Barthelme's work, as Trachtenberg notes, also borrows from abstract art in *subtracting* from conventional form.

Architecture, the cinema, and music—particularly jazz and country—all gave him what painters call "scrap," but it was painting that allured him, painting that showed him what the writer could do, and painting that he tried to emulate in voicing the heretofore unvoiced. He said so himself, that the advantage painting gave was "physicality."

Collage he found useful. His story "See the Moon" is verbal collage, and a later parody, "Eugénie Grandet," further refines the scheme with its use of textual fragments, disconnected dialogue, letters, a drawing, an illustration, and a photograph. Some of these were genuine, the "sort of thing," he said, that "Dos Passos did in the Newsreels [and] what Joyce did in various ways."

This study, examining and evaluating an elaborate cross-section of Barthelme's work, including his novels, will show that what mattered was method. Gass explains, "Putting end to end and next to next is Barthelme's method, and in Barthelme, blessed method is everything." Barthelme says, "The *way* things are done is crucial, as the inflection of a voice is crucial. The change of emphasis from the what to the how seems to me to be the major impulse in art since Flaubert, and it's not merely formalism, it's not at all superficial, it's an attempt to reach truth, and a very rigorous one."

To the extent that he succeeded, how poetic intuition accounts for part of his success. In "Not-Knowing," he echoes Mallarmé:

> Art is not difficult because it wishes to be difficult, rather because it wishes to be art. However much the writer might long to be, in his work, simple, honest, straightforward, these virtues are no longer available to him. He discovers that in being simple, honest, straightforward, nothing much happens: he speaks the speakable, whereas we are looking for the as-yet unspeakable, the as-yet unspoken. (116–17)

Considering his effort as a whole, it could be said that he was trying to renew and safeguard the language by creating a wildlife preserve for the mind and language of the meditative narrative with work that could not be parodied or reduced, writing that would remain fresh and alive with all its meanings undiminished and open-ended.

M.T.H.
28 July 2000

WORKS CITED IN THE FOREWORD

Barth, John. *Further Fridays: Essays, Lectures, and Other Nonfiction 1984–94.* Boston: Little Brown, 1995.

——. "Thinking Man's Minimalist: Honoring Barthelme." *The New York Times Book Review*: 3 September 1989.

Barthelme, Donald. "Not-Knowing." *Major Writers of Short Fiction.* Ed. Ann Charters Boston: Bedford Books of St. Martin's P, 1993. 113–24.

Eco, Umberto. *Postscript to The Name of the Rose.* San Diego: Harcourt Brace Jovanovich, 1984. 65–72.

Gass, William H. *Fiction and the Figures of Life.* Boston: David R. Godine, 1979.

Trachtenberg, Stanley. *Understanding Donald Barthelme.* Columbia, South Carolina: U of South Carolina P, 1990.

Wilde, Alan. *Middle Grounds: studies in contemporary American fiction.* Philadelphia: U of Pennsylvania P, 1987.

1   SPEAKING THE HERETOFORE UNSPEAKABLE

Jackdaw-like, Donald Barthelme was sometimes called, for selecting the artistic material that glittered most. His response on one occasion: "I weep and tear my hair. And disagree." Later in the same interview, he adds: "Actually I think the jackdaw business is a function of appearing in the *New Yorker* regularly. People read the fiction with after-images of Rolls Royces and Rolexes still sizzling in their eyes. . . . One is gilded by association" (O'Hara 190–91). The proof is in the pun: it's jackdaw-like.

His story "On Angels" opens with the line, "The death of God left the angels in a strange position" (*60 Stories* 135), a statement that might leave the reader in the lurch as well.

The second line of the story, "They were overtaken suddenly by a fundamental question," charts a path, but before he reveals the question, he poses another: "How did they *look* at the instant the question invaded them, flooding the angelic consciousness, taking hold with terrifying force?" Then he returns to the fundamental question—the thesis of this piece: "What are angels?"

Next, like a video director switching between cameras, he's trying to characterize the angels' reaction to the Demise: "New to questioning, unaccustomed to terror, un-skilled in aloneness, the angels (we assume) fell into despair." But this is a transition, bringing us back to his first order of business, answering what are angels.

He invokes scientist-theologian Emanuel Swedenborg who claims to have spoken with numerous angels and painstakingly documented their statements.

> Angels look like human beings, Swedenborg says. "That angels are human forms, or men, has been seen by me a thousand times." And

again: "From all of my experience, which is now of many years, I am able to state that angels are wholly men in form, having faces, eyes, ears, bodies, arms, hands, and feet. . . " But a man cannot see angels with his bodily eyes, only with the eyes of the spirit. (135)

The seventh paragraph of the story refers to a 1957 paper by Joseph Lyons, "The Psychology of Angels," in which

[t]he former angelic consciousness has been most beautifully described. . . Each angel, Lyons says, knows all that there is to know about himself and every other angel. "No angel could ever ask a question, because questioning proceeds out of a situation of not knowing, and of being in some way aware of not knowing. An angel cannot be curious; he has nothing to be curious about. He cannot wonder. Knowing all that there is to know, the world of possible knowledge must appear to him as an ordered set of facts which is completely behind him, completely fixed and certain and within his grasp. . ." (136).

Consciousness of self, awareness of all, omniscience—Donald Barthelme must be talking about Postmodernist literature. This seraphical disquisition is really about Postmodernist writers, which is made clear (as clear as it's going to get) in the 10th paragraph when the question "What are angels?" is answered with an elliptical statement that is marvelously empty, especially considering that the writer of these words was a non-practicing Catholic: "An angel is what he does" (137).

Barthelme finishes this up the way he does other stories, with his rendering of the Ethel Barrymore[1] exit line that there isn't any more. The angels go about investigating new roles for themselves: the "mode of lamentation," which is to say, "silence, in contrast to the unceasing chanting of Glorias that had been their former employment. But it is not in the nature of angels to be silent" (137).

---

[1] Closing Thomas Raceward's play *Sunday* in 1904 Miss Barrymore added the signature curtain line: "That's all there is, there isn't any more."

And not in the nature of Italo Calvino, flinging language into the face of silence, of truth and untruth, and of death itself. By linking the piece to the cerebral, philosophical Calvino, Barthelme makes the connection to all Postmodern fictionists. They're the angels, trying to determine what to do.

The angels consider chaos: "There were to be five great proofs of the existence of chaos, of which the first was the absence of God. The other four could surely be located."

Chaos would be an ambitious area of specialization. "The work of definition and explication could, if done nicely enough, occupy the angels forever, as the contrary work has occupied human theologians. But there is not much enthusiasm for chaos among the angels" (137).

Next contemplated is refusal. The angels "would remove themselves from being, not be. The tremendous dignity that would accrue to the angels by this act was felt to be a manifestation of spiritual pride. Refusal was refused" (137).

Silence, chaos, and refusal rejected, the story closes with a coda:

> I saw a famous angel on television; his garments glistened as if with light. He talked about the situation of angels now. Angels, he said, are like men *in some ways*. The problem of adoration is felt to be central. He said that for a time the angels had tried adoring each other, as we do, but had found it, finally, "not enough." He said they are continuing to search for a new principle. (137)

Many readers are put off by such work as this, by its seeming lack of customary linear development or concentration that would bring about development. The reality here is its own, and Trachtenberg certainly agrees:

> Symmetrical in shape, recurrent in structure, these fictions neutralize time and space, dissolving not only the nature of reality but the aesthetic process by which it is conventionally made to yield some sort of meaning. What remains is something outside the narrator's perception, something, in fact, that establishes its reality precisely because it does not take its shape from the person or voice through which it is viewed. (8)

And even though Barthelme repeats common speech patterns and uses objects of popular culture, he distorts this domain by "distilling and flattening its images so that in place of a textured world everything becomes a prop" (Trachtenberg 8).

"On Angels," a small story of 14 paragraphs, is the work of one ardently dedicated to showing his readers a good time and who in much of his prose, to borrow his own words in praise of Mallarmé, "shakes words loose from their attachments and bestows new meanings upon them, meanings that point not toward the external world but toward the Absolute, acts of poetic intuition" ("Not-Knowing" 116–17).

He believed this, and it is evident in the previously mentioned five interviews, conducted in the 1971, 1980, 1981, 1982, and 1988. The 1981 conversation, J. D. O'Hara's piece for that year's Paris Review, is probably the most significant. John Barth, in his 3 September 1989 *New York Times Book Review* eulogy to Barthelme, says of the O'Hara effort, "Donald worked *hard* on that anything-but-spontaneous interview—as wise, articulate and entertaining a specimen as can be found in the Paris Review's long, ongoing series of shoptalks. He worked hard on all his printed utterance, to make it worth his and our whiles" (9).

MAKE IT NEW

His artistic influences, from several genres, shifted over the years. Asked about them, he would list writers, Venturi, artists, filmmakers, and several musicians. There was a time he listened constantly to rock (Klinkowitz 52). O'Hara observes: "Music is one of the few areas of human activity that escapes distortion in your writing. An odd comparison: music is for you what animals were for Céline" (184). Barthelme does not dispute this, saying that when he was growing up,

> There were a lot of classical records in the house. Outside, what the radio yielded up was mostly Bob Wills and the Texas

Playboys; I heard him so much that I failed to appreciate him,
failed to appreciate country music in general. Now I'm very fond
of it. I was interested in Jazz and we used to go to black clubs to
hear people like Erskine Hawkins who were touring—us poor little
pale little white boys were offered a generous sufferance, tucked
away in a small space behind the bandstand with an enormous
black cop posted at the door. In other places you could hear people
like the pianist Peck Kelly, a truly legendary figure, or Lionel
Hampton or once in a great while Louis Armstrong or Woody
Herman. I was sort of drenched in all this. After a time a sort of
crazed scholarship overtakes you and you can recite band rosters
for 1935 as others can list baseball teams for the same year.
(O'Hara 184–85)

Asked what was to be learned from it, he says, "The interest and the drama were
in the formal manipulation of the rather slight material. And they were heroic
figures, you know, very romantic" (185). And from this, he says, came at least
one character, Hokie Mokie of Pass Christian, Mississippi in "The King of Jazz"
(*60 Stories* 354–58). With music, he explains, it was "[m]aybe something about
making a statement, about placing emphases within a statement or introducing
variations. You'd hear some of these guys take a tired old tune like 'Who's Sorry
Now?' and do the most incredible things with it, make it beautiful, literally make
it new" (O'Hara 185).

Make it new—another writer had all but shouted this from the rooftops,
and here Barthelme, restating it just so, is alluding to Ezra Pound. He is
mentioned in Barthelme's 1963 essay "After Joyce," and shows up in *The King*,
making his anti-Semitic broadcasts from Rome (7), but is conspicuous by his
absence elsewhere. If ever there was a Barthelme character, it would be Pound,
with his red hair and cape and view of himself as a troubadour poet (Simpson vii),
walking the London streets in the early years of the 20th century—so goes the
Ford Madox Ford account—"with the step of a dancer, making passes with a cane
at an imaginary opponent. He would wear trousers made of green billiard cloth, a
pink coat, a blue shirt, a tie hand-painted by a Japanese friend, an immense
sombrero, a flaming beard cut to a point, and a single, large blue earring" (qtd. in

Simpson 9). He abounded in eccentricities and contradictions—calling for "hard light, clear edges" (Simpson 41), counseling the artist, "Go in fear of abstractions" (Simpson 36), and every step of the way violating these exhortations. In *Guide to Kulchur* Pound says, Barthelme-like, "Let the reader be patient. I am not being merely incoherent" (29). And Barthelme sounds Pound-like talking about rendering messiness and making it coherent.

The common ground here appears expansive. Both were seeking something similar—centrality in contemporary consciousness—and Hassan names Pound one of the "antecedents" of Postmodernism (589).

Make it new. To O'Hara's question, "Why this constant invocation of the word 'new?'" Barthelme's reply is, "It equates with being able to feel something rather than with novelty per se, it's a kind of shorthand for discovery." Asked about his well-known constant scrutiny of his style and methodology, his explanation is, "You isolate aspects of the process, look at them separately, worry about this and then worry about that. It's like a sculptor suddenly deciding to use rust" (189).

Brans asked him in 1982 about creating new forms and getting rid of older ones. "I don't think I've gotten rid of anything," he says. "People seem to regard it as a process of destruction in some sense, but I don't see why the two things can't exist." Not abolishing, he insists, "Just choosing to do different things." It's a common perception, he says, that "as each new movement of art comes along, the people involved traditionally issue manifestoes, claiming that everything has been overturned, and a whole new order is extant. . . . But I have issued no manifestoes. Just doing my number" (127).

His number, in his time, with an awareness of others. In 1974 he answered a name-your-influences request with: "Among writers of the past, I'd list Rabelais, Rimbaud, Kleist, Kafka, Stein, and Flann O'Brien. Among living writers, Beckett, Gass, Percy, García Márquez, Barth, Pynchon, Kenneth Koch, John Ashbery, Grace Paley" (Klinkowitz 53). In 1981 he was telling O'Hara,

"Gass, Hawkes, Barth, Ashbery, Calvino, Ann Beattie . . . Walker Percy . . . Handke, Thomas Bernhard, Max Frisch, [García] Márquez" (186).

Who would he name as his spiritual ancestors? "They come in assorted pairs. Perelman and Hemingway. Kierkegaard and Sabatini. Kafka and Kleist. Kleist was clearly one of Kafka's fathers. Rabelais and Zane Grey. The Dostoyevsky of *Notes from Underground.* A dozen Englishmen." And the Surrealists, "both painters and poets. A great many film people, Buñuel (best known his 1972 *The Discreet Charm of the Bourgeoisie*) in particular. It's always a stew, isn't it? Errol Flynn ought to be in there somewhere, and so should Big Sid Catlett, the drummer. . . ." Asked why Errol Flynn is included, he says, "Because he's part of my memory of Sabatini, Sabatini fleshed out. He was in the film version of *Captain Blood,* and *The Sea Hawk.* He should have done *Scaramouche* but Stewart Granger did it instead, as I recall." Barthelme describes own story, "Captain Blood," as a "pastiche of Sabatini, not particularly of that book but all of Sabatini. You are reminded, I hope, of the pleasure Sabatini gives you or has given you." As to his short fiction, "The piece is in no sense a parody, rather it's very much an *hommage.* An attempt to present, or recall, the essence of Sabatini. Also it hopes to be an *itself*" (O'Hara 187–88). Are these influences or, with the exception of Hemingway, the scrap of artists?

In 1982 he said, "Hemingway taught us all. First, wonderful things about rhythm, his sentence rhythms, and wonderful things about precision, and wonderful things about being concise. His example is very, very strong." *The Sun Also Rises* is "[h]is best novel by far. Although I like *A Farewell to Arms* and the stories—just beautiful. I certainly can't be said to write like Hemingway, but he certainly is an influence" (Brans 128).

Trachtenberg attempts a comparison:

> Where Hemingway's understatement relied on an underlying depth or iceberg solidity to account for the unexpressed emotion, the lack of inflection—a change in pitch or tone to indicate relationships— in Barthelme's fiction is invested with little psychological or historical density. Nothing goes on beneath events; little seems to

have occurred before they are set in motion. His fiction tends toward the fixed moment rather than the flowing stream. It accords precedence to quantity over quality. It is an acknowledgment rather than a process of discovery—an acknowledgment, above all, that the narrative voice shares the attitudes and anxieties of the characters. (21)

Film "bombarded" Barthelme from age six, with "the effect of teaching me what waste is"; and "as with painting, film has shown us what not to pursue. The movies provide a whole set of stock situations, emotions, responses that can be played against. They inflect contemporary language. One uses this" (McCaffery 42).

Above all else, what structured and shaped his fiction came out of his residence in New York. The process that led him to relocate started in 1959, when he was named director of Houston's Contemporary Arts Museum. Three years later, he met Harold Rosenberg, an art critic, who with Thomas Hess, was planning an art-literary magazine, *Location*, to be published in New York City (Trachtenberg 3). Rosenberg and Hess asked Barthelme to come to New York as managing editor, he accepted, and the three became lifelong friends. Barthelme took up residence in a Greenwich Village place "whose stimulating if messy vitality he compared to the collages of the artist Kurt Schwitters" (Trachtenberg 3). Collage techniques began to show up in Barthelme's writing. In the story "See the Moon," he has the narrator grumbling that collage artists "can pick up a Baby Ruth wrapper on the street, glue it to the canvas (in the *right place*, of course, there's that), and lo! people crowd about and cry, 'A real Baby Ruth wrapper, by God, what could be realer than that.' Fantastic metaphysical advantage" (*60 Stories* 98). The advantage, he explains, is the painting's physicality (McCaffery 36). "See the Moon" itself is verbal collage, and Barthelme's later parody, "Eugénie Grandet," shows further refinement of the scheme with its use of textual fragments, disconnected dialogue, letters, a drawing, an illustration, and a photograph (*60 Stories* 236–44). Regarding certain of the graphical elements being genuine—old woodcuts and the like, he points out that

> This sort of thing is of course what Dos Passos did in the Newsreels, what Joyce did in various ways. I suppose the theater has the possibility of doing this in the most immediate way. I'm on the stage and I suddenly climb down into the pit and kick you in the knee. That's not like writing about kicking you in the knee, it's not like painting you being kicked in the knee, because you have a pain in the knee. (McCaffery 37)

Roe says, "[H]is move to New York City in 1962 initiated his most significant tutelage. According to Barthelme, over scandalous lunches and on afternoon jaunts to galleries, museums, and studios, Tom Hess and Harold Rosenberg schooled him in both abstract expressionism and the poetics of Ashbery, Koch, and Schuyler" (30).

Hess and Rosenberg died in 1978. During the O'Hara interview, Barthelme recalls that "Tom Hess used to say that the only adequate criticism of a work of art is another work of art. It may also be the case that any genuine work of art generates new work" (186). Later in the conversation, he mentions Rosenberg's book *The Tradition of the New* (189) and talks about misunderstanding an artist's work:

> I remember going through a very large Barnett Newman show years ago with Tom Hess and Harold Rosenberg . . . and I walked through the show like a certifiable idiot, couldn't understand their enthusiasm. I admired the boldness, the color and so on but inwardly I was muttering "wallpaper, wallpaper, very fine wallpaper but wallpaper." I was wrong, didn't get the core of Newman's enterprise, what Tom called Newman's effort toward the sublime. Later I began to understand. One doesn't take in Proust or Canada on the basis of a single visit. (200)

Roe continues:

> After his mentors' deaths in 1978, Barthelme continued these pilgrimages, particularly to SoHo and East Village galleries. He also wrote catalog introductions for Mary Boone and Rauschenberg shows. To Rauschenberg's collages and found

objects, he attributes in part the complex structures of his most perplexing stories. By saddling a goat with a tire, Rauschenberg invested otherwise ordinary objects with magic: no one can resolve the contradictions of that odd merger. Barthelme hoped to conjure words with equal sorcery. (30–31)

This goat, discussed in "Not-Knowing," is another key understanding Barthelme.

> Any work of art depends upon a complex series of interdependencies. If I wrench the rubber tire from the belly of Rauschenberg's famous goat to determine, in the interest of a finer understanding of same, whether the tire is a B. F. Goodrich or a Uniroyal, the work collapses, more or less behind my back. I say this not because I find this kind of study valueless but because the mystery worthy of study, for me, is not the signification of parts but how they come together, the tire wrestled over the goat's hind legs. Calvin Tomkins tells us in *The Bride and the Bachelors* that Rauschenberg himself says that the tire seemed "something as unavoidable as the goat." To see both goat and tire as "unavoidable" choices, in the context of art-making, is to illuminate just how strange the combinatorial process can be. Nor was the choice a hasty one; Tomkins tells us that the goat had been in the studio for three years and had appeared in two previous versions (the final version is entitled "Monogram") before it met the tire. (119)

Barthelme's work, Trachtenberg says, as in "abstract painting is significant for what it subtracts from conventional form" (7). In the story "Engineer-Private Paul Klee Misplaces an Aircraft Between Milbertshofen and Cambrai, March 1916," the artist Klee does not know what happened to the aircraft. Where it had been, tied down to a flatcar and covered with canvas, is a space: "there is only a puddle of canvas and loose rope" (*40 Stories* 82). Because nothing can ever bring it back, "[r]eason dictates the solution. I will diddle the manifest. With my painter's skill which is after all not so different from a forger's, I will change the manifest. . ." (83). The story ends with Klee saying, "I eat a piece of chocolate. I am sorry about the lost aircraft but not overmuch. The war is temporary. But drawings and chocolate go on forever" (84).

The page as canvas, functioning by subtraction instead of addition, was an idea of the Symbolists. In the essay "Spatial Form in Modern Literature," Frank discusses the zeal of Mallarmé' "to create a language of 'absence' rather than of presence—a language in which words negated their objects instead of designating them" (13). When Pound said, "Go in fear of abstractions," he was speaking as an Imagist, chastising the Symbolists for being throwbacks to Romanticism (Simpson 35).

In the Brans interview Barthelme, asked if there was "a dramatic moment in which the form of a Barthelme short story emerged," replies, "Yes, but it was a 10-year moment." His explanation is telling:

> I was trying to do something different. Well, I was trying to make art, and I didn't want to do it as Cheever does it, although I admire very much what Cheever does—but that's what Cheever does. I was trying to do something else. I suppose I was trying—in the crudest statement—I was trying to make fiction that was like certain kinds of modern painting. You know, tending toward the abstract. But it's really very dicey in fiction, because if you get too abstract it just looks like fog, for example. (Brans 126–27)

Make it new is not without peril, of course. Cicero had it right: "Nothing quite new is perfect." By the time of Roe's 1988 interview Barthelme's position has changed: "'Make it new' as a battle cry seems naïve today, a rather mechanical exhortation. If a piece of writing is of this time, of a particular time, that seems quite enough to ask of it." To Roe's insistence that "there's something exciting about the new," he will only grant "there's a frisson there, but perhaps nothing lasting." One wonders if he felt this way five years earlier, or when the change occurred. He finishes up telling Roe: "I think it has to do with seeing something done well. Above all, we like to see something done well, and in writing, when it's done really well, there's always an element of freshness which is probably an aspect of craft but may appear to be an aspect of time, may appear to be 'the new'" (107).

ARCHITECTURAL ATTITUDES AND POP CULTURE

To O'Hara's observation that Barthelme's "feelings about the new are ambivalent," the response is:

> I'm ever-hopeful, but remember that I was exposed early to an almost religious crusade, the Modern movement in architecture, which, putting it as kindly as possible, has not turned out quite as expected. The Bauhaus, Miës van der Rohe and his followers, Frank Lloyd Wright and his followers, Le Corbusier, all envisioned not just great buildings but an architecture that would engender a radical improvement in human existence. The buildings were to act on society, change it in positive ways. None of this happened and in fact a not insignificant totalitarian bent manifested itself. (190)

His entire childhood, he explains,

> was colored to some extent by [being] enveloped in Modernism. The house we lived in, which he'd designed, was Modern and the furniture was Modern and the pictures were Modern and the books were Modern. He gave me, when I was 14 or 15, a copy of Marcel Raymond's *From Baudelaire to Surrealism,* I think he'd come across it in the Wittenborn catalogue. The introduction is by Harold Rosenberg, whom I met and worked with 16 or 17 years later, when we did the magazine *Location* in New York.

Dynamics were wrought by the other parent as well.

> My mother studied English and drama at the University of Pennsylvania, where my father studied architecture. She was a great influence in all sorts of ways, a wicked wit. (O'Hara 184)

In an interview the following year, he goes into more detail about his father: "It was an attitude toward his work." The elder Barthelme's training in architecture, he continues, had been "entirely in the Beaux Arts tradition. No whiff of modernism was allowed to penetrate the Penn architecture school at that time. And he got out of school and suddenly the whole world changed for him . . . he went through a complete reversal—his world turned upside down, in a way." At this time, the late 1920s and early 1930s, a Modern building was a rarity. "So, his task was to do an entirely new thing, which was contrary to his training in important ways. And he did it with great enthusiasm, with great zest, and he did it very, very well." The home in which he and his brothers grew up, "was a terrible anomaly amidst all the houses around it. It looked weird, although it was a very beautiful house, somewhat similar to Miës's Tugendhat house.[2] And then, inside the house, the furniture was all Aalvar Aalto stuff. It was not like real furniture, in a way . . . this stuff was weird-looking." Yet, by the 1980s, he points out, there was "Aalto-derived furniture in airport waiting rooms, for example. But it was unusual then, and it had to have been, both visually and spiritually, important" (Brans 121–22).

Enter Venturi, in 1966, with what he called his "gentle manifesto," *Complexity and Contradiction in Architecture.* The book is a broadside against mainstream Modernism and its glass-and-steel boxes that had gone up all over the postwar world. To Miës's celebrated dictum, "less is more," Venturi countered with, "Less is a bore" (Arnason 691). At this writing in mid 2000, *Complexity and Contradiction* is still widely read and considered pertinent, despite the prevailing belief that architectural Postmodernism was but one more flash in the pan (Filler 10).

It is in the structures of Venturi that a visual equivalent to Donald Barthelme's fiction can be found (Trachtenberg 19), or even a metaphor for his philosophical and artistic resistance to Modernist aesthetics. Barthelme would echo Venturi in stating preferences, as in one interview when he discusses always looking for "a particular kind of sentence, perhaps more often the awkward than the beautiful. A back-broke sentence is interesting." This, he explains, would be a sentence beginning with some phrase along the lines of "It is not clear that . . . ." This, he says, "is clearly clumsy but preparing itself for greatness of a kind. A way of backing into a story—of getting past the reader's hard-won armor." The

---

[2] Built in Brnö, Czechoslovakia in 1930 by the German-American architect, Ludwig Miës van der Rohe and badly damaged in World War II (Poole 147).

full sentence, stated earlier in the same interview, demonstrates this: "'It is not clear that Arthur Byte was wearing his black corduroy suit when he set fire to the Yale Art and Architecture Building in 1968" (McCaffery 34). At the end of the story "Sentence," the narrator says that the sentence is "a structure to be treasured for its weakness, as opposed to the strength of stones (*40 Stories* 163). Venturi will be discussed later in this study.

Barthelme, asked if he himself ever considered going into architecture, gave a predictable reply: "No, I always wanted to be a writer, even when I was small" (Brans 122).

In the O'Hara interview he was questioned about literary biography, if he thought his biography might help clarify his stories and novels: "Not a great deal. There's not a strong autobiographical strain in my fiction. A few bits of fact here and there." One of these is a passage in the story "See the Moon?" and there is an appearance by his grandparents in a piece he does not name. The conversation moves to his grandfather: "He was a lumber dealer in Galveston and also had a ranch on the Guadalupe River not too far from San Antonio, a wonderful place to ride and hunt, talk to the catfish and try to make the windmill run backward" (183). In Barthelme's last weeks of life—he died July 23, 1989 in Houston—he again refers to these visits to his grandfather's spread (Trachtenberg 4).

Asked a year earlier about using pop culture materials such as the Phantom of the Opera, King Kong, and Snow White in his fiction, he responds: "Relatively few of my stories have to do with pop culture, a very small percentage really. What's attractive about this kind of thing is the given—you have to do very little establishing, can get right to the variations" (McCaffery 42).

In the Roe conversation he says, "There's a consistent social concern in my stories from the 1960s to the present. Tends to be slipped in while your attention is directed toward something else . . . but it's there." He explains that he was not talking about direct political satire found in his collection *Guilty Pleasures* "but rather an obligato, always present in everything" (110).

Barthelme always felt that he benefited from the times in which he wrote.

> [T]he worse the political situation, the more stimulating it is for the writer. Most of the pieces in *Guilty Pleasures* were written during the Nixon administration, when things were so egregiously wrong that we were on a continual ladder of amazement and outrage. The Reagan administration probably did as much damage to the country but in ways more difficult to identify. A great advantage Central European writers have is the absolutely miserable political conditions in their home countries. (Roe 110)

John Barth in his *New York Times Book Review* eulogy says,

> I have heard Donald referred to as essentially a writer of the American 1960's. It may be true that his alloy of irrealism and its opposite is more evocative of that fermentatious decade, when European formalism had its belated flowering in North American writing, than of the relatively conservative decades since. But his literary precursors antedate the century, not to mention its 60's, and are mostly non-American. "How come you write the way you do?" a Johns Hopkins apprentice writer once asked him. "Because Samuel Beckett already wrote the way *he* did," Barthelme replied. He then produced for the seminar his "short list": five books he recommended to the attention of aspiring American fiction writers. No doubt the list changed from time to time; just then it consisted of Rabelais's *Gargantua and Pantagruel,* Laurence Sterne's *Tristram Shandy,* the stories of Heinrich von Kleist, Flaubert's *Bouvard and Pécuchet* and Flann O'Brien's *At Swim-Two-Birds*— a fair sample of the kind of nonlinear narration, sportive form and cohabitation of radical fantasy with quotidian detail that mark his own fiction. He readily admired other, more "traditional" writers, but it is from the likes of these that he felt his genealogical descent.

He saw himself connected to certain contemporaries as well.

> Similarly, though he tsked at the critical tendency to group certain writers against certain others "as if we were football teams"—praising these as the true "post-contemporaries" or whatever, and consigning those to some outer darkness of the passé—he freely acknowledged his admiration for such of his "teammates," in those critics' view, as Robert Coover, Stanley Elkin, William Gaddis, William Gass, John Hawkes, Thomas Pynchon and Kurt Vonnegut, among others.

"Among others" includes Barth, who was present at this gathering:

> A few springs ago, he and his wife, Marion, presided over a memorable Greenwich Village dinner party for most of these and their companions (together with his agent, Lynn Nesbit, whom Donald called "the mother of postmodernism"). In 1988, on the occasion of John Hawkes's academic retirement, Robert Coover impresarioed a more formal reunion of that team, complete with readings and symposia, at Brown University. Donald's throat cancer had by then already announced itself—another, elsewhere, would be the death of him—but he gave one more of his perfectly antitheatrical virtuoso readings.

Barth's perceptions of the group:

> How different from one another those above-mentioned teammates are! Indeed, other than their nationality and gender, their common inclination to some degree of irrealism, and to the foregrounding of form and language, and the circumstance of their having appeared on the literary scene in the 1960s or thereabouts, it is not easy to see why their names should be so frequently linked (or why Grace Paley's, for example, is not regularly included in that all-male lineup). But if they constitute a team, it has no consistently brighter star than the one just lost. (9)

Barth calls Barthelme "a thinking man's—and woman's—Minimalist," and praised his "urbane and urban semi-Surrealism" and "superb verbal art" (9).

But readers are turned away by some of his efforts. He explains, "There's always the tension between losing an audience and doing the odd things you might want to try. The effort is always to make what you write nourishing or useful to readers. You do cut out some readers by idiosyncrasies of form. I regret this" (McCaffrey 42).

Asked by O'Hara what starts off a story, Barthelme says,

> It's various. For instance, I've just done a piece about a Chinese emperor, the so-called First Emperor, Ch'in Shih Huang Ti.[3] This came directly from my wife's research for a piece she was doing on medical politics in Chinatown—she had accumulated all sorts of material on Chinese culture, Chinese history, and I began

---

[3] "The Emperor," *60 Stories* 429–32.

picking through it, jackdaw-like. This was an emperor who surrounded his tomb with that vast army of almost full-scale terra cotta soldiers the Chinese discovered just a few years ago. The tomb, as far as I know, has yet to be fully excavated, but the scale of the discovery gives you some clear hints as to the size of the man's imagination, his ambition. (192)

Charles Newman, who views Donald Barthelme as a Modernist, although one of a new generation, makes this observation:

The hallmark of a Barthelme story, for example, whatever its quality, is that it is *essentially unparodyable*. Think of the consequences of that—anticipating every objection in its very rhythms, a work of art which will not yield to further mimicry. Within its own context it can only be imitated: neither totally assimilated nor challenged; the *ne plus ultra* of daemonic irony, the end of the road of interiority. (Newman 79)

Could Newman have been thinking of the opening to Barthelme's story "Grandmother's House," a layered construction of *Little Red Riding Hood, The Three Little Pigs, Beauty and the Beast,* and perhaps the news section of *The New York Times*?

—Grandmother's house? What? Landmark status? What? She's been eating? What? Strangers? She's been eating strangers? Sitting up in bed eating strangers? Hey? Pale, pink strangers? Zut! Lithium? What? They're giving her lithium? Hey? She's a what? Wolf? She's a wolf? Gad! Second opinion? Hey? She's a wolf. Well, Well, then. And Grandfather? What? Living with a stranger? Hey? A pale, pink stranger? Abominable! What's her name? What? What? Belle? Tush. BelleBelleBelleBelleBelle no I don't like it. Well if Grandmother's house has landmark status that means we can't build the brothel, right? Can't build the brothel, right? No brothel, right? Damn and damn and damn. (*60 Stories* 450)

18

WORKS CITED IN THE CHAPTER

Arnason, H. H. *History of Modern Art*. New York: Harry N. Abrams, 1986.

Barth, John. "Thinking Man's Minimalist: Honoring Barthelme." *The New York Times Book Review*, 3 September 1989: 9.

Barthelme, Donald. *40 Stories*. New York: Penguin, 1989.

——. "Not-Knowing." *Major Writers of Short Fiction: Stories and Commentaries*. Ed. Ann Charters. Boston: Bedford Books of St. Martin's Press. 113–24.

——. *60 Stories*. New York: Penguin, 1993.

——. *The King*. New York: Penguin, 1992.

Brans, Jo. "Embracing the World: An Interview with Donald Barthelme." *Southwest Review*, Spring 1982.

Filler, Martin. Rev. of *Iconography and Electronics upon a Generic Architecture: A View from the Drafting Room*, by Robert Venturi. *The New York Review* 23 October 1997: 10.

Frank, Joseph. "Spatial Form in Modern Literature." *The Widening Gyre: Crisis and Mastery in Modern Literature*. New Brunswick: Rutgers UP, 1963. 3–62.

Hassan, Ihab. "Toward a Concept of Postmodernism." *Postmodern American Fiction: A Norton Anthology*. Ed. Paula Geyh, Fred G. Leebron, and Andrew Levy. New York: Norton, 1998. 586–95.

Klinkowitz, Jerome. "Donald Barthelme." *The New Fiction: Interviews with Innovative American Writers*. Joe David Bellamy, ed. Urbana: U of Illinois P, 1974.

McCaffery, Larry. "An Interview with Donald Barthelme." *Anything Can Happen: Interviews with Contemporary American Novelists.* Ed. Thomas LeClair and McCaffery. Urbana: U of Illinois P, 1983. 32–44.

Newman, Charles. *The Post-Modern Aura: The Act of Fiction in an Age of Inflation.* Evanston: Northwestern U P, 1985.

O'Hara, J. D. "Donald Barthelme: The Art of Fiction LXVI." *The Paris Review* 1981.

Pound, Ezra. *Guide to Kulchur.* New York: New Directions, 1952.

Roe, Barbara. *Donald Barthelme: A Study of the Short Fiction.* New York: Twayne, 1992.

Simpson, Louis. *Three on the Tower: The Lives and Works of Ezra Pound, T. S. Eliot and William Carlos Williams.* New York: William Morrow, 1975.

Trachtenberg, Stanley. *Understanding Donald Barthelme.* Columbia, South Carolina: U of South Carolina P, 1990.

Not a Postmodernist but a Latter Day Modernist.

Newman is not alone in saying this, but still, Barthelme's work seems far afield from Lawrence and Fitzgerald. Not so much from Faulkner, though, when Barthelme's *The Dead Father* is considered. Or from Joyce. Perspective is needed, a vantage with sufficient altitude to see, jackdaw-like, just where along the continuum the work of Donald Barthelme and the other Postmodernists is located.

Eco says, "Actually, I believe that postmodernism is not a trend to be chronologically defined, but, rather, an ideal category—or, better still, a *Kunstwollen*, a way of operating. We could say that every period has its own postmodernism, just as every period would have its own mannerism (66).

Newman takes the position that the "'Post-Modern' is neither a canon of writers, nor a body of criticism, though it is often applied to literature of, roughly, the last twenty years [1965–1985]"(5). He believes that "the Modern and the Post-Modern share an unbroken (and largely unexamined) aesthetic tradition," that "Modernism in its heroic phase is a retrospective revolt against a retrograde mechanical industrialism," whereas "Post-Modernism is an ahistorical rebellion without heroes against a blindly innovative information society" (10).

Postmodernism is the result of information inflation, he contends, pointing out that most books in today's typical library were published during the last 30 years, that more novels were published during these three decades than in any comparable period, and that during the 1930s some 8,000 titles were published annually, while today that number is 55,000 (Newman 9).

Annie Dillard holds that the term *Postmodernist* bears the same burden as its sibling term, *Post-Impressionist* (19). She too believes that Modernism is alive and well: "The historical Modernists are dead: Kafka, Joyce, Faulkner, and also Biely, Gide, Malraux, Musil, Woolf. But one could argue—and I do—that diverse contemporary writers are carrying on, with new emphases and further developments, the Modernists' techniques." Dillard names contemporary writers who are reaching "various interesting extremes": Jorge Borges, Vladimir Nabokov, Samuel Beckett, Robert Coover, John Barth, John Hawkes, William Burroughs, Donald Barthelme, Thomas Pynchon, Rudolph Wurlitzer, Thomas M. Disch, Alain Robbe-Grillet, Jonathan Baumbach, William Hjortsberg, Flann O'Brien, Italo Calvino, Tommaso Landolfi, Julio Cortázar, Manuel Puig, Elias Canette, and Carlos Fuentes (20; Dillard's order of names). A late list of Barthelme's is narrower —Barth, William Gass, Hawkes, Coover, William Gaddis, Pynchon, himself, Calvino, Peter Handke, and Thomas Bernhard (his order)—but he would have added others ("Not-Knowing" 116).

Both Dillard and Newman view Barthelme as part of a new generation of Modernists. Alan Wilde says, "[T]he time has come to recognize that contemporary fiction does not lend itself to the kinds of binary oppositions that are the subject of Thomas Pynchon's anathematizations and that, in mapping the literary present, all too easily divide the field between the realistic and the metafictional." Wilde sees "a middle ground where many of today's best writers, Barthelme among them, position themselves." Midfiction, he says, "carves out for itself a more equivocal but also a more various space in which to bring the world into being." He believes that "thematically, stylistically, and structurally, Barthelme's work, or much of the best of it, belongs with the tertium quid of midfiction" (Wilde 166).

Considered in a later chapter are these and other arguments, not excluding opposing views such as those of John C. Gardner in *On Moral Fiction,* an effort

Barthelme calls "clearly an attempt at a Saint Valentine's Day Massacre" (Brans 129).

On the Modernism issue Barthelme himself was ambiguous: "Critics, of course, have been searching for a term that would describe fiction after the great period of modernism—'postmodernism,' 'metafiction,' 'surfiction,' and 'superfiction.' The last two are terrible; I suppose 'postmodernism' is the least ugly, most descriptive" (McCaffrey 38).

As to the metafiction label, "I don't have any great enthusiasm for fiction-about-fiction. It's true that in 1965 I put that questionnaire in the middle of *Snow White*. But I haven't done that much in that direction since. I think I've actually been fairly restrained" (38). He tells Roe in 1988 that his writing is not metafiction but rather "a way of dealing with reality, an attempt to think about aspects of reality that have not, perhaps, been treated of heretofore. I say it's realism, bearing in mind Harold Rosenberg's wicked remark that realism is one of the 57 varieties of decoration" (108).

In the early 1960s, Philip Roth suggested that certain writers started down another road when reality began outstripping fiction's ability to amaze the reader. Barthelme agrees.

> I do think something happened in fiction about that time, but I'd locate it differently—I think writers got past being intimidated by Joyce. Maybe the reality that Roth was talking about was instrumental in this recognition, but I think that people realized that one didn't have to repeat Joyce (if that were even possible) but could use aspects of his achievement. (McCaffery 38)

On occasion, Barthelme would jump off his fence to fuel the fires of the Postmodernism controversy. A comic letter he invented for "Not-Knowing" says, at once tongue-in-cheek and point-blank: "Postmodernism is dead. A stunning blow, but not entirely surprising. I am spreading the news as rapidly as possible, so that all of our friends who are in the Postmodernism 'bag' can get out of it before their cars are repossessed and the insurance companies tear up their policies"(114).

And what is to be made of his ranking in this statement? "Sad to see Postmodernism go (and so quickly!). I was fond of it. As fond, almost, as I was of its grave and noble predecessor, Modernism. But we cannot dwell in the done-for" (114).

Movements come, movements go, he goes on. "So many, so many. . . . Surrealism gone, got a little sweet toward the end, you could watch the wine of life turning into Gatorade. Sticky. Altar Poems—those constructed in the shape of an altar for the greater honor and glory of God—have not been seen much lately: missing and presumed dead" (115).

The letter finishes—"What shall we call the New Thing, which I haven't encountered yet but which is bound to be out there somewhere? Post-Postmodernism sounds, to me, a little lumpy"—essentially where it began. "I've been toying with the Revolution of the Word, II, or the new Revolution of the Word. . . . It should have the word 'new' in it somewhere. The New Newness? Or maybe the Post-New? It's a problem. . . . If we're going to slap a saddle on this rough beast, we've got to get moving" (115).

His comments that follow the faux letter loosen the rein somewhat: "If I am slightly more sanguine than Alphonse [signature on the letter] about postmodernism, however dubious about the term itself and not altogether clear as to who is supposed to be on the bus and who is not, it's because I locate it in relation to a series of problems, and feel that the problems are durable ones" (115–16).

Clearly, a change reveals itself with that statement.

Near the end of "Not-Knowing" another statement answers questions about his own work: "Art cannot remain in one place, a certain amount of movement, up, down, across, even a gallop toward the past, is a necessary precondition" (123).

If Barthelme is finally deemed a late Modernist, how will the realist issue be resolved? Wilde is emphatic: "That Barthelme is not a realist, no one, I think, will deny" (166).

Barthelme, defining *realism* in its broadest sense, fidelity to being, says: "I take the position that I am writing realistic fiction. Everybody's a realist. Every writer is offering a true account of the activities of the mind." One example, he says, "At the end of ["The Leap"] the two men are talking about the passage of time, and so on, and they begin reciting a list of beautiful things, and one guy says, 'Like when you see a woman with red hair, I mean really red hair.' And there's a list—and each detail is a real thing—an accurate report" (Brans 132). Among the items: "Small boys bumping into small girls, purposefully. . . . Gravediggers working in the cool early morning. . . . A walk in the park. . . . Another day when the singing sunlight turns you every way but loose. . . . When you accidentally notice the sublime." The list finishes with, "A wedding day. . . . A plain day" ("The Leap" 385). He says, "I think the distinction between who's a realist and who's a surrealist is slightly specious. By definition, one can only offer the activity of the individual mind, however it's notated. It's all realism"(Brans 132).

William Gass in his 1979 book *Fiction and the Figures of Life* says that Barthelme has positioned himself "in the center of modern consciousness. Nothing surrealist about him, his dislocations are real, his material quite actual. Radio, television, movies, newspapers, books, magazines, social talk: these supply us with our experience. Rarely do we see trees, go meadowing, or capture crickets in a box" (100).

Bytes and bites of pointless fact assail Gass, he says. "Put end to end like words, my consciousness is a shitty run of category errors and non sequiturs. Putting end to end and next to next is Barthelme's method, and in Barthelme, blessed method is everything" (100).

Concerning method, Barthelme explains, "The *way* things are done is crucial, as the inflection of a voice is crucial. The change of emphasis from the what to the how seems to me to be the major impulse in art since Flaubert, and it's not merely formalism, it's not at all superficial, it's an attempt to reach truth, and a very rigorous one." This approach is unsuitable for producing a Ten Commandments, he says, "but we already have that. And the attempt is sufficiently skeptical about itself. In this century there's been much stress placed not upon what we know but on knowing that our methods are themselves questionable—our Song of Songs is the Uncertainty Principle" (O'Hara 199-200). This is undoubtedly a core truth in Donald Barthelme's work.

THE WAY AND THE HOW

Surveying Barthelme's work as a continuum, a beginning can be located: his first *New Yorker* publication, a dialogue that appeared in the March 2, 1963 issue under the title "L'Lapse" with subtitle "A Scenario for Michelangelo Antonioni." This nearly forgotten Italian film director ascended to fame in 1959 with an overrated picture called *L'Avventura*. Barthelme's piece, which he characterized as a "standard" *New Yorker* parody (Klinkowitz 48), targets cinema reviewers who praised the movie.

In "L'Lapse" the film critic Marcello is sitting by a fountain with his friend Anna. Her statement, "I was bored," displeases him, and he says, "The point is, you were bored *in a certain way.* Like brilliantly." Still, Anna says, it was "a little . . . slow." Marcello responds: "*Of course* it was slow. I mean it had a certain slow beauty. A sort of visual rubato. On the other hand, it was obscure and baffling. . . . I mean you can't just say you were *bored,* for God's sake" (173).

The dialogue contains several allusions and one direct reference to the great Italian director Federico Fellini, whose surreal *La Dolce Vita* (1960) and *8-1/2* (1963) were generating shock waves at this time. Of significance in Barthelme's otherwise undistinguished early effort is that "L'Lapse" *sounds* like a

Fellini film, and evokes what is probably the best known scene from his classic *La Dolce Vita*, when another Marcello (played by Marcello Mastroianni) tries halfheartedly and unsuccessfully to seduce Sylvia (Anita Ekberg) at Rome's Fountain of Trevi.

Capturing voice always was one of Barthelme's singular strengths. "I listen to people talk, and I read. I doubt that there has ever been more jargon and professional cant—cant of various professions and semi-professions—than there is today," he says. "I remember being amazed when I was in basic training, which was back in the early 50s, that people could make sentences in which the word *fucking* was used three times or even five times" (McCaffery 38).

Another early influence is the Texas drawl to which he was exposed throughout boyhood. A remarkable example is found in "Two Hours to Curtain," a monologue that originally appeared as part of "Flying to America" in the December 4, 1971 *New Yorker*. The story is light on substance but has the basso-profundo, monotone, public-address-system voice of a Texas rodeo announcer down pat. This is recognizable Texas drawl, perhaps the voice a young Donald Barthelme used to hear at performances of the Houston Fat Stock Show & Rodeo in the late 1940s:

> A big battle dance in Rogers, Tennessee! These country boys, despised and admired, know what they're about. The way they pull on their strings—the strings of their instruments, and the strings of their fates. Bringing up the bass line here, inserting "fills" there, in their expensive forty-dollar Western shirts and plain ordinary nine-dollar jeans. Four bands are competing, and the musicians backstage are unscrewing their flasks and tasting the bourbon inside, when they are not lighting their joints and pipes and hookahs. Meanwhile they're looking over the house, the Masonic Temple, a big pile of stone erected in 1928, and wondering whether the wiring will be adequate to the demands of their art. The flasks and joints are being passed around, and everyone is wiping his mouth on his sleeve. (193)

And in this parody of the Ford-Carter debates, the voice of President Jimmy Carter in "The Great Debate," appearing in the May 3, 1976 *New Yorker*:

"He who hath Love in his heart hath in his heart Love. . . . If a man hath the entire Sun Belt and two Disneylands also and hath not Love, then it may be said he hath the moola but heedeth not the call of the mullah, which is Love" (84–85).

In a late work entitled "More Zero: A Novel of Los Anomies" that appeared in the *New Yorker* on July 7, 1986, three years before his death, is a voice unlike any he ever attempted—an 18-year-old effeminate male, *ultra* upscale southern California: "Ashley picks me up in one of the two red BMWs her mother gave her for her birthday. She's wearing sunglasses and a Wheat Chex T-shirt and tight jeans and says that DataLife will be at Pablo's tonight and do I want to go. I'm doing a line of coke off the rearview mirror as she drives and it's sort of tricky and I don't answer her." He mentions that he is totally exhausted after having spent the previous night in a game of Old Maid with friends Kimberly and Griff. "We stop at Fanfare and the valet guy takes the car and nods at Ashley and he looks like some guy I'd seen at Oliver's house in Bel Air the night Oliver OD'd, tan with short blond hair, but Ashley apparently doesn't know him." After some business with the menu and the waiter, "I get really tense and go into the men's room and there's this guy there, too tan with short blond hair, who looks like a guy who was at Spago with Kimberly the night Kimberly totaled her new black Porsche. . . ." In the wrecked car were designer shirts she'd bought for another acquaintance on the occasion of his release from Cedars-Sinai Hospital—detail piled upon detail except why Kimberly's friend was in the hospital, which does not seem important, anyway. "I nod to him and say 'Hey dude,' he doesn't respond, just looks at me. He's holding a big can of Ajax and rubbing Ajax into his gums but I know it isn't Ajax, it's probably Comet or Ajax cut with Comet; the guy slides to the floor and I step over him and wash my hands and put some water on my face and go back to Ashley" (179). This voice, a composite of mass media advertising and the *Los Angeles Times* society page, is reminiscent of Joyce's Gerty MacDowell in *Ulysses*.

Some of Barthelme's best collage is in dialogues, and these appear throughout his work. Asked if they are *Beckett-y*, he responds: "Certainly they couldn't exist without the example of Beckett's plays. But I have other fish to fry" (O'Hara 197).

More dialogues appear in the 1979 *Great Days* than in other collections, which, he explains, "really came from trying the dialogues in *The Dead Father* between the two women. That was the impulse. The dialogues in *The Dead Father* are really collections of non sequiturs, intended to give the novel another kind of voice, to provide a kind of counter-narration to the main narration" (Brans 134).

Dialogues have to be finely tuned, he says: "The opportunities are those of poetry without the stern responsibilities. Dialogues are rather easy to write but there are some fine points. The sentence rhythms are rather starkly exposed, have to be weirdly musical or you send the reader off to Slumberland posthaste" (O'Hara 197).

He was drawn to dialogue, he says, because "It's stripped, allows essentials to be dealt with in a rather pure way. . . . I don't have to get people in and out of doors. I don't have to describe them. I don't have to put them in a landscape. I just deal with their voices" (Brans 133–34).

By "essentials" he means relationships between voices and between the words themselves, his own examples being Phillipe Sollers in his book *Paradis*, and some of Gertrude Stein's work: "I'm talking about a pointillist technique, where what you get is not adjacent dots of yellow and blue which optically merge to give you green but merged meanings, whether from words placed side by side in a seemingly arbitrary way or phrases similarly arrayed, bushels of them." It is, he says, "a North Sea to be explored" (O'Hara 197–98). In "Not-Knowing" he continues on this: "The combinatorial agility of words, the exponential generation of meaning once they're allowed to go to bed together, allows the writer to surprise himself, makes art possible, reveals how much of Being we haven't yet encountered" (121–22). The seventh line of his 1978 story "The Leap" is a fine example: "I am cheered by the wine of possibility and the growing popularity of light" (379).

"The Leap" and his 1985 "Basil from Her Garden" are as enigmatic as any of his writings, to be sure, but "Not-Knowing" illuminates both, and together the three form a centerpiece of his work, a place of transformation on his landscape. The title "Not-Knowing" refers to what is essential to art, the search for knowingness that moves the artist in different directions to discover the what and the how (113–14)

In "The Leap" the dialogue of two speakers carries the narrative, and space and time are not apparent. The conversation, yet another series of verbal collages, begins and ends with the same speaker, but as it progresses, a surprising change occurs. To differentiate the pair, they are designated here as One and Two.

"The Leap" opens with One saying, "Today we make the leap to faith." *To faith*, in the version printed in *60 Stories*, not *of.* In the Charters anthology we see "leap of faith," but lines 108, "This being an example of the leap away from faith," and 109, "You can jump either way" (383) confirm the correctness of *to*. Leaping *to* faith—faith being the belief in "that which is" (OED)—is suggestive of *Faustus*, the final act, as the good doctor awaits his deliverance:

> *O lente, lente currite, noctis equi!*
> [Slowly, slowly run, O horses of the night!]
> The stars move still, time runs, the clock will strike,
> The devil will come, and Faustus must be damn'd.
> O, I'll leap up to my God! Who pulls me down?
> *Faustus*, V. ii.140–43

Two asks: "We're really going to do it? At last?" One insists they have "[s]pent too much time fooling around. Today we do it,"and Two responds: "I don't know. Maybe we're not ready?"

One won't be swayed; today's the day. To his exhortation that they first examine their consciences, Two says, "I am a double-minded man. Have always been a double-minded man." One amplifies this: "Each examining his own conscience, rooting out, naming, remembering and re-experiencing every last little cank and wrinkle. Root and branch" ("The Leap" 379). Two's pair of minds would appear to be in conflict, like old and new brains, reptilian and mammalian, housed in one cranium.

Both One and Two are effusive in their praise of the human mind. One declares: "[I]n my judgment the finest of our human achievements," and Two assents: "Much the finest. I can think of nothing remotely comparable" (382).

They digress, they backpedal, they stall for time. Anything to distance them from the precipice from which the leap would be made. They praise the human voice, trees, flowers, population growth, zero population growth, a glass of water. One says, "I like people better than plants, plants better than animals, paintings better than animals, and music better than animals," but insists, "I *respect* the animals. I *admire* the animals" (380). One relates an anecdote: "Did I ever tell you about that time when I was in Saigon and Cardinal Spellman came to see us at Christmas and his plane was preceded by another plane broadcasting sacred music over the terrain? Spraying the terrain as it were with sacred music?" (382).

Each diversion helps draw a distinction between the two, and at the same time counteracts it, closing the gap between them. Their exchanges suggest that the two voices actually represent one mind. Beyond the OED definition of *double-minded*, "having two minds" and "undecided or wavering in mind," the term can be taken literally as the hemispheres of one cerebrum communicating with each other.

That One and Two are of the same mind is revealed when Two shows One an itemized hospital bill belonging to a female acquaintance who recently tried to do herself in. They review some of the hospital charges, and Two, who produced out the bill in the first place, asks One for the total of the bill. One reads it out.

Two says, "And the acquaintance?" One answers: "She's well." Two responds: "This being an example of the leap away from faith."

Did they change roles? Or does one know what the other knows, because they're the same person? With this switch, the story has a compelling symmetry, like that of the human face and body. Right and left correspond but do not necessarily match.

The above passage also brings to light the object of *faith* in "The Leap." It is imparted in the line from Two about the acquaintance, her attempted suicide "being an example of the leap away from faith." If self-annihilation is "the leap away"—that is, a leap to a state of nonexistence—then *faith*, the belief in "that which is," can only refer to the self.

Two, who starts out wanting to postpone the leap until later, invokes Isaiah 30:21: "This is the way, walk ye in it." In the biblical context these are God's words, instructing the prophets: "While from behind, a voice shall sound in your ears: 'This is the way; walk in it,' when you would turn to the right or to the left." Barthelme's catalog of worldly goods—ferns, jazz, wine—listed in the story appears to allude to the next verse, 22: "And you shall consider unclean your silver-plated idols and your gold-covered images; you shall throw them away like filthy rags to which you say, 'Begone!'"

The piece ends with One, originally so intent on making the leap to faith, telling Two: "Can't make it, man. . . . Can't make it. I am a double-minded man. . . . An incorrigibly double-minded man" (385).

Quite like Barthelme himself, quoted saying that he is fated to deal in mixtures. "It's a habit of mind, a perversity. Tom Hess used to tell a story, maybe from Lewis Carroll, I don't remember, about an enraged mob storming the palace shouting 'More taxes! Less bread!' As soon as I hear a proposition I immediately consider its opposite. A double-minded man—makes for mixtures" (O'Hara 195).

"Basil from Her Garden" begins with an apparent therapy session between two male speakers whom Barthelme has designated Q and A, as in his 1970 stories "The Explanation" and "Kierkegaard Unfair to Schlegel." In the latter, however, Q says, "I am not your doctor" (167), while in "Basil" the implication is quite clear that his task is to counsel A. Unlike the double-minded individual of "The Leap," the interrogator Q and the respondent A are entirely separate. In the course of both "Basil" and "Kierkegaard" Barthelme the ironist defeats the static roles associated with the question-and-answer format. Q's initial Socratic questioning gives way to rambling and self-doubt, and he ends up receiving reassurance from A. Near the end of "Basil" Q says, "I'm only a bit depressed, only a bit" (106).

In "The Leap" Two says, "We are but poor lapsarian futiles whose preen glands are all out of kilter"(384), and in "Basil" Q the questioner declares: "A new arrangement of ideas, based upon the best thinking, would produce a more humane moral order, which we need" (106). In "The Leap," seven lines after Two's "lapsarian futiles" statement, One quotes Kierkegaard: "Purity of heart is to will one thing," whereupon Two comes back with: "No. Here I differ with Kierkegaard. Purity of heart is, rather, to will several things, and not know which is the better, truer thing, and to worry about this, forever" (384).

The absolute, the immutable, versus that which is not. What is beneficial about the mutable and its attendant ambiguity is that it forces us to find answers for ourselves, thereby defining us and dignifying us by our efforts. For the double-minded Barthelme, the ambiguities of existence pervaded both life and art, and in "Not-Knowing" he echoes this: "Problems are a comfort. Wittgenstein said of philosophers that some of them suffer from 'loss of problems,' a development in which everything seems quite simple to them, and what they write becomes (I'm quoting) 'immeasurably shallow and trivial.'" It applies to writers too, he says (116). "Problems, in part, define the kind of work the writer chooses to do, and are not avoided but embraced. A writer, says Karl Kraus, is a man who can make a riddle out of an answer"(118).

That some readers will be excluded by design, he says again, is inescapable. "Art is not difficult because it wishes to be difficult, rather because it wishes to be art" (116). The writer is forced into "having the mind move in unanticipated directions" (113).

Painters know that accuracy is not truth, and the same applies to crafting with the written word. "However much the writer might long to be, in his work, simple, honest, straightforward, these virtues are no longer available to him. He discovers that in being simple, honest, straightforward, nothing much happens: he speaks the speakable, whereas we are looking for the as-yet unspeakable, the as-yet unspoken" (116–17).

Barthelme describes his approach to the short story as a "process of accretion. Barnacles growing on a wreck or a rock. I'd rather have a wreck than a ship that sails. Things attach themselves to wrecks. Strange fish find your wreck or rock to be a good feeding ground; after a while you've got a situation with possibilities"(McCaffery 34). This is a Venturi idea.

Again, double-mindedness: messy is good. He explains: "To render 'messy' adequately, that is, to the point that you are enabled to feel it—I don't want you to recognize that it's there, it should, ideally, frighten your shoes. . . . What should be emphasized is that one proceeds by way of particulars" ("Not-Knowing 121).

On the preceding page of "Not-Knowing" the question is posed, "In what sense is the work about the world?" (120), and partially answered with the statement, "The world enters the work as it enters our ordinary lives, not as a world-view or system but in sharp particularity" (121). The rest of the answer comes later: "I suggest that art is always a meditation upon external reality rather than a representation of external reality" (123).

Meditation can be—sometimes should be—*messy*. He tells O'Hara how messiness is achieved: "De Kooning can do 'messy' by making a charcoal stroke over paint and then smudging same with his talented thumb—in prose the same gesture tends to look like simple ineptitude. De Kooning has a whole vocabulary of bad behavior which enables him to set up the most fruitful kinds of contradictions" (199). In "Not-Knowing," Barthelme says, "To render 'messy' adequately, that is, to the point that you are enabled to feel it . . . I would have to be more graphic than the decorum of the occasion allows. What should be emphasized is that one proceeds by way of particulars." The words he would use to render *messy*

> are not inert, rather they're furiously busy. We do not mistake the words *the taste of chocolate* for the taste of chocolate itself but neither do we miss the tease in *taste,* the shock in *chocolate.* Words have halos, patinas, overhangs, echoes. The word *halo,* for instance, may invoke St. Hilarius, of whom we've seen too little lately. The word *patina* brings back the fine pewtery shine on the saint's halo. The word *overhang* reminds us that we have, hanging over us, a dinner date with St. Hilarius, that crashing bore. The word *echo* can call up Echo herself, poised like the White Rock girl on the overhang of a patina or a halo—infirm ground, we don't want the poor spirit to pitch into the pond where Narcissus blooms, eternally; they'll bump foreheads, or maybe other parts closer to the feet, a scandal—There's chocolate smeared all over Hilarius's halo, messy, messy. . . (121).

In terms of life and morality, human existence itself is messy in both "Leap" and "Basil." Two's mention of humanity's lapsarian state reflects his feeling of loss over the perfect order of Eden. Throughout "Basil" Q embraces this view of the prelapsarian ideal, while A's Eden could just as easily be the mundane garden of his covetable neighbor, Rachel, and its steady supply of a mundane culinary herb. There is the unmistakable ring of Rabelais[4] here, surveying an imperfect world: "Oh thrice and four times happy those who plant cabbages."

A wonders about off-world, if there is intelligent life in such places, if Christ visited each one, and if so, what about "these guys on these other planets,

---

[4] *Gargantua and Pantagruel,* Book IV

these life forms, maybe they look like boll weevils or something, on a much larger scale of course, were they told that they shouldn't go to bed with other attractive six-foot boll weevils arrayed in silver and gold and with little squirts of Opium behind the ears?" It makes no sense, he says. "But of course our human understanding is imperfect" ("Basil" 103).

A's, however, is better. "I don't think God gives a snap about adultery. This is just an opinion, of course. . . . You think about this staggering concept, the mind of God, and then you think He's sitting around worrying about this guy and this woman at the Beechnut TraveLodge? I think not" (104).

But he is accepting of change and, when it comes, seems always ready ride it out: "I sometimes think of myself as a person who . . . could have done something else, it doesn't matter what particularly. Just something else" (102). He is open to dreaming, bow hunting, saving the environment, committing adultery (101), joining the CIA (102), and choosing to covet or not covet his neighbor's wife (105); whereas Q can accept nothing less than the absolute, Kierkegaard's purity of heart. "Ethics has always been where my heart is," Q says. "Moral precepting stings the dull mind into attentiveness." In response to A's statement, "I obey the Commandments, the sensible ones," Q says, "He critiques us, we critique Him" (106).

THE ELSEWHERE

Q wants *otherness,* which Barthelme first addresses in his 1964 story, "Florence Green is 81." The male narrator tells us that a group of friends has gathered at Florence Green's for dinner: "The old babe is on a kick tonight: *I want to go to some other country,* she announces. Everyone wonders what this can mean. But Florence says nothing more: no explanation, no elaboration, after a satisfied look around the table bang! she is asleep again" (3).

Later in the evening, he reflects on what she said: "Florence I have decided is evading the life-issue. She is proposing herself as more unhappy than she really is. She has in mind making herself more interesting. She is afraid of boring us. She is trying to establish her uniqueness. She does not really want to go away" (13).

She wakes up briefly. "What about Casablanca? Santa Cruz? Funchal? Málaga? Valetta? Iráklion? Samos? Haifa? Kotor Bay? Dubrovnik? "I want to go to some *other* place," Florence says. "Somewhere where *everything is different*"(14). In other words, elsewhere.

As the evening ends, the narrator has a change of heart: "*I want to go somewhere where everything is different. A* simple, perfect idea. The old babe demands nothing less than total otherness" (15).

He leaves, gets into his blue Volkswagen: "No one has taken Florence seriously, how can anyone with $300 million be taken seriously? But I know that when I telephone tomorrow, there will be no answer. Iráklion? Samos? Haifa? Kotor Bay? She will be in none of these places but in another place, a place where *everything is different"* (16).

In "The Sandman," 1972, a letter from Susan's boyfriend to her psychiatrist, the question is posed—"What do you do with a patient who finds the world unsatisfactory?"—and answered, with characteristic Barthelme pessimism of the time—"The world *is* unsatisfactory; only a fool would deny it" (197).

In "Basil" A and Q regard adultery very differently. For A, it is otherness. He tells Q that he spends most of his free time in adultery, that the Seventh Commandment is wrong, possibly a mistranslation from the Aramaic (101–103), but even so, when he commits adultery, "There's a certain amount of guilt attached. I feel guilty. But I feel guilty even without adultery. I exist in a morass of guilt. There's maybe a little additional wallop of guilt but I already feel so guilty that I hardly notice it. . . ." Then he widens the scope of this: "I hazard that it is not guilt so much as it is inadequacy. I feel that everything is being nibbled away, because I can't *get it right"* (103).

But in fact he is getting it right because he accepts the messiness of things, whereas Q's efforts at seeking control and thereby imposing order are futile. Q worries about what he calls "last things": "Myself, I think about being just sort of a regular person, one who worries about cancer a lot, every little thing a prediction of cancer, no I don't want to go for my every-two-years checkup because what if they find something?" He ruminates over what finally might kill him, and the when and how. "I wonder about my parents, who are still alive, and what will happen to them. This seems to me to be a proper set of things to worry about. Last things" (103–104).

In the closing of the story Q says that he sometimes imagines himself in the pest control business, driving "a small white truck with a red diamond-shaped emblem on the door and a white jumpsuit with the same emblem on the breast pocket" (106). The badge identifies Q as the instrument of order, and after he goes through a customer's $300,000 home with his silver canister of poison, pumping and spraying alongside the emblems of their lives, his status is reconfirmed: "The young wife escorts me to the door, and, in parting, pins a silver medal on my chest and kisses me on both cheeks. Pest Control!" (107).

A says, "Yes, one could fit in that way. It's finally a matter, perhaps, of fit. Appropriateness. Fit in a stately or sometimes hectic dance with nonfit. What we have to worry about" (107).

Q's response is characteristic: "It seems to me that we have quite a great deal to worry about. Does the radish worry about itself in this way? Yet the radish is a living thing. Until it's cooked"(107). Which is to say, worrying about mutability makes no difference.

In the closing lines of "Basil" Q is beset with fresh doubts. It is the fear that's been nagging him all along, that the only absolute is disorder, because the radish is certain to be cooked. Q is looking outside himself for answers, for transcendence, while A looks within. It is in the self that he can find harmony with "nonfit," be it in a "stately or sometimes hectic dance."

Q — Transcendence is possible.
A — Yes.
Q — Is it possible?
A — Not out of the question.
Q — Is it really possible?
A — Yes. Believe me. (107)

For Q, transcendence is God. For A, it is self. Therefore, transcendence is possible for A. He can say, Trust Me, but Q, of course, cannot and never will.

Most of "Basil from Her Garden" appears as chapters in *Paradise*, Barthelme's third novel. In this thoughtful book, he appears to have distanced himself from the cynicism and irony of his other work. Unfortunately, *Paradise* has received little recognition so far and at this writing was out of print.[5] In the novel, A is the 53-year-old narrator, Simon, who calls Q "a shrink." Q later refers to himself as a doctor.

Paradise, considered in another chapter of this study, reflects a change in approach evident in certain of Barthelme's later work. There are fewer jokes, he admits (McCaffrey 44) and not as much anger (Brans 131). The shift can be connected to statements in "Not-Knowing":

Style, he says, is not a matter of choice: "One does not sit down to write and say: Is this poem going to be a Queen Anne poem, a Biedermeier poem, a Vienna Secession poem or a Chinese Chippendale poem? Rather it is both a response to constraint and a seizing of opportunity. Very often a constraint is an opportunity."

A definition follows: "Style is of course *how*, and the degree to which *how* has become *what* since, say, Flaubert is a question that men of conscience wax wroth about, and should." To illustrate, he put himself in the chair of a bistro musician who, "ridden by strange imperatives," likes to score golden oldies for banjulele, a banjo-uke hybrid. "Let us suppose that I am the toughest banjulele player in town and that I have contracted to play 'Melancholy Baby' for six hours

---

[5] Hardback Putnam's 1986, paperback Penguin 1987.

before an audience that will include the four next-toughest banjulele players in town." What he cannot do should be obvious: "I am not going to play 'Melancholy Baby' as written. Rather I will play something that is parallel, in some sense, to 'Melancholy Baby,' based upon the chords of 'Melancholy Baby,' made out of 'Melancholy Baby,' having to do with 'Melancholy Baby'—commentary, exegesis, elaboration, contradiction" (122–23).

That his interpretation includes commentary and exegesis guarantees that information and knowledge of feeling will be supplied, because, after all, "Melancholy Baby" is *about* feeling.

His banjulele creation takes on a new perspective: "The interest of my construction, if any, is to be located in the space between the new entity I have constructed and the 'real' 'Melancholy Baby,' which remains in the mind as the horizon that bounds my efforts" (123).

Wilde says that as the word *horizon* suggests, "not-knowing depends as much upon the fluid boundaries of consciousness (what 'bounds my efforts') as upon consciousness itself" (168).

Barthelme's conclusion comes in a new paragraph: "This is, I think, the relation of art to the world. I suggest that art is always a meditation upon external reality rather than a representation of external reality." Again, accuracy is not at issue here. "If I perform even reasonably well, no one will accuse me of not providing a true, verifiable, note-for-note reproduction of 'Melancholy Baby' [because] it will be recognized that this was not what I was after" (123)

And here, in the next sentence of the same paragraph, is a signal revelation: "Twenty years ago I was much more convinced of the autonomy of the literary objects than I am now, and even wrote a rather persuasive defense of the proposition that I have just rejected, that the object is itself world" (123).

It finishes with this explanation: "Beguiled by the rhetoric of the time—typified by a quite good magazine called *It Is,* published by the sculptor Philip Pavia—I felt that the high ground had been claimed and wanted to place my scuffed cowboy boots right there. The proposition's still attractive. What's the right answer? Bless Babel" (123).

This "rejection" is typically double-minded. The "persuasive defense" he mentions appears in "After Joyce,"[6] published in 1963: "Interrogating older works, the question is: what do they say about the world and being in the world? But the literary object is itself 'world' and the theoretical advantage is that in asking it questions you are asking questions of the world directly." This is not writerly ventriloquism, but "rather, a stunning strategic gain for the writer. He has in fact removed himself from the work, just as Joyce instructed him to do. The reader is not listening to an authoritative account of the world delivered by an expert . . . but bumping into something that is *there,* like a rock or a refrigerator" (13).

In the 1988 conversation with Roe he says,

> Both positions are defensible. The first idea, that the artwork is an object in the world in much the same way a dog biscuit or a mountain is an object in the world, is an effort to deny that the artwork is a rendering or a copy of the world. The second position attempts to be a little clearer about the relation between art and the world, and I ended by saying that art is a meditation about the world rather than a reproduction of some aspect of the world. The two ideas are not directly contradictory. The relevant line is "Art is a true account of the activity of the mind." I don't mean to suggest that that's all art is, merely that this is a place to begin. The statement does take into account the controversy about the truth value of art, does a bit of work there. (108)

Not directly contradictory—but indirectly. He had every right to change his mind, even to want it both ways.

CHOICES

This leads back to the question of the material itself and how the writer can best array it: "In the streets outside the apartment, melting snow has revealed

---

[6] The essay and *Finnegans Wake* will be considered in the next chapter of this study.

a choice assortment of decaying et cetera. Furthermore, the social organization of the country is untidy; the world situation is in disarray. How do I render all this messiness, and if I succeed, what have I done?" ("Not-Knowing" 121). As in "Basil" and its array of the ordinary, "[t]he world enters the work as it enters our ordinary lives, not as a world-view or system but in sharp particularity," one example being a snowball with a résumé inside (121). "The prior history of words is one of the aspects of language the world uses to smuggle itself into the work," he explains. "If words can be contaminated by the world they can also carry with them into the work trace elements of the world which can be used in a positive sense. We must allow ourselves the advantages of our disadvantages" (122).

The urban imagery of New York, Barthelme's home until his death in 1989, accounts for at least some of his fictional vision. He says in the 1971 interview that the city itself, with all the rubbish, "can be regarded as a collage, as opposed to, say, a tribal village in which all of the huts (or yurts, or whatever) are the same hut, duplicated" (Klinkowitz 51). On several subsequent occasions he mentions the collages of German artist Kurt Schwitters, known for his *Merz* (trash) constructions: "At moments, in New York, I like all the filth on the streets, it reminds me of Kurt Schwitters. Schwitters used to hang around printing plants and fish things out of waste barrels, stuff that had been overprinted or used during make-ready, and he'd employ this rich accidental material in his collages." Barthelme says that everything in a large Schwitters show he saw reminded him of New York: "Garbage in, art out" (O'Hara 202).

Gass makes his call: "Dreck, trash, and stuffing: these are his principal materials. But not altogether. There is war and suffering, love and hope and cruelty." Barthelme's hope, Gass quotes him as saying, is that all of it "'will merge into something meaningful.' But first he renders everything as meaningless as it appears to be in ordinary modern life by abolishing distinctions and putting everything in the present." This, of course, describes his process, and, like the horizon that he says bounds his efforts, "[h]e constructs a single plane of truth, of relevance, of style, of value—a flatland junkyard—since anything dropped in the dreck *is* dreck, at once, as an uneaten porkchop mislaid in the garbage" (101). Cleverness, the cheap joke, the topical—all are dreck, according to Gass. "Who knows this better than Barthelme, who has the art to make a treasure out of trash, to see *out* from inside it, the world as it's faceted by colored jewelglass?" (103).

Always, Barthelme took instruction from painting: "Painters, especially American painters since the Second World War, have been much more troubled, beset by formal perplexity, than American writers." Painters, for this reason, have "been a laboratory for everybody. Some new attitudes have emerged. What seems clear is that if you exacerbate a problem, make it worse, new solutions are generated. Ad Reinhardt is an example. Barnett Newman, proceeding by subtraction, or Frank Stella rushing in the other direction" (O'Hara 188–89).

He tells McCaffery that painting of the 1960s and especially of the 1970s "really pioneered for us all the things that it is not necessary to do. Under the aegis of exploring itself, exploring its own means or the medium, painting really did a lot of dumb things that showed poets and prose writers what might usefully not be done." He goes on to explain: "I'm thinking mostly of conceptual art, which seems to me a bit sterile. Concrete poetry is an example of something that is, for me, not very nourishing, though it can be said to be exploratory in the way that a lot of conceptual art is exploratory" (37). In "See the Moon" the narrator says painters have a "fantastic metaphysical advantage" (98). Which is, Barthelme says, "[t]he physicality of the medium—there's a physicality of color, of an object present before the spectator, which painters don't have to project by means of words. I can peel the label off [a] bottle of beer . . . and glue it to the canvas and it's there." So he gathers dreck in the form of phrases, clichés, rhythms, and "sung to and Simonized, they're thrown into the mesh." Dos Passos did this, he says, and it is to a T "what Joyce did in various ways" (McCaffery 36–37).

WORKS CITED IN THE CHAPTER

Barthelme, Donald. *60 Stories*. New York: Penguin, 1993.

——. "After Joyce." *Location*. New York: Longview Foundation, 1963. 13–16.

——. "Basil from Her Garden." Charters 101–07.

——. "Florence Green is 81." *Come Back, Dr. Caligari*. Boston: Little, Brown, 1964.

——. "The Great Debate." Herzinger 83–87.

——. "Kierkegaard Unfair to Schlegel." *60 Stories* 160–68.

——. "L'Lapse." Herzinger 172–77.

——. "The Leap." *60 Stories* 379–85.

——. "More Zero: A Novel of Los Anomies." Herzinger 178–80.

——. "Not-Knowing." Charters 113–24.

——. *Paradise*. New York: Putnam's, 1986.

——. "The Sandman." *60 Stories* 191–98.

——. "See the Moon?" *60 Stories* 97–107.

——. "Two Hours to Curtain." Herzinger 193–95.

Brans, Jo. "Donald Barthelme: Embracing the World." *Southwest Review* 67 (Spring 1982).

Charters, Ann, ed. *Major Writers of Short Fiction*. Boston: St. Martin's P, 1993.

Dillard, Annie. *Living by Fiction.* New York: Harper & Row, 1988.

Eco, Umberto. *Postscript to The Name of the Rose.* San Diego: Harcourt Brace Jovanovich, 1984. 65–72.

Gass, William H. *Fiction and the Figures of Life.* Boston: David R. Godine, 1979.

Herzinger, Kim, ed. *The Teachings of Don B.: Satires, Parodies, Fables, Illustrated Stories, and Plays of Donald Barthelme.* New York: Turtle Bay Books, 1992.

Klinkowitz, Jerome. "Donald Barthelme." *The New Fiction: Interviews with Innovative American Writers.* Ed. Joe David Bellamy. Urbana: U of Illinois P, 1974. 45–54.

Marlowe, Christopher. *The Tragical History of Doctor Faustus: From the Quarto of 1604.* In *The Plays of Christopher Marlowe.* Ernest Rhys, ed. London: J. M. Dent, 1929. 120–158.

McCaffery, Larry. "An Interview with Donald Barthelme." *Anything Can Happen: Interviews with Contemporary American Novelists.* Ed. Thomas LeClair and McCaffery. Urbana: U of Illinois P, 1983. 32–44.

Newman, Charles. *The Post-Modern Aura: The Act of Fiction in an Age of Inflation.* Evanston: Northwestern U P, 1985.

O'Hara, J. D. "Donald Barthelme: The Art of Fiction LXVI." *Paris Review* 80 (1981). 181–210.

Roe, Barbara. *Donald Barthelme: A Study of the Short Fiction.* New York: Twayne, 1992.

Wilde, Alan. Middle Grounds: studies in contemporary American fiction. Philadelphia: U of Pennsylvania P, 1987.

3   JOYCE AS POSTMODERNIST

Given that "the Joyce of *Ulysses* was a Modernist," says John Barth, "had the Joyce of *Finnegans Wake* already moved on to Postmodernism?" (119).

Umberto Eco maps the way to the *Wake*:

> Look at Joyce. The *Portrait* is the story of an attempt at the Modern. *Dubliners*, even if it comes before, is more modern than *Portrait*. *Ulysses* is on the borderline. *Finnegans Wake* is already postmodern, or at least it imitates the postmodern discourses: it demands, in order to be understood, not the negation of the already said, but its ironic rethinking. (68)

Charles Newman views the *Wake,* published in 1939, as a marker: "Contemporary writing exists uneasily between an establishment which sees *Finnegans Wake* as the end of a genre, or a beginning, and an adolescent culture which sees itself as somehow sprung fully armed from the void. . . (98).

William Gass calls the *Wake* "a work of learning. It can be penetrated by stages. It can be elucidated by degrees. It is a complex, but familiar, compound. One can hear at any distance the teeth of the dogs as they feed on its limbs" (87). Successful art, he explains, "dare not be pure. It must be able to invite the dogs. It must furnish bones for the understanding" (80).

Some of Barthelme's work seems to acknowledge the *Wake* and "The Dead," the final and longest story in *Dubliners,* 1914. Details accumulate and accrete in several Barthelme short stories and in his novel *The Dead Father* as they do in the *Wake.* The novel *Paradise* is circular, the first chapter a continuation of the last. Simon of *Paradise* has parallels to Gabriel of "The Dead": both are in the process of reaching out of themselves, and the two works make extensive use of clashes of incidents. Apart from this, "The Dead," a Modern masterpiece and one of the finest works in the language, is considered here in some detail primarily because it is Joyce stripped down, without all the layering found in the *Wake,* and thus can serve as a standard. As to Barthelme, he was no Joycean scholar, but he knew the work and viewed it as an obstacle course to be crossed.

"The Dead" opens straightforwardly, in media res with the commotion of guests arriving for the annual Christmas dinner dance at the house of the Morkan sisters, including their favorite nephew, Gabriel Conroy, and his spouse Gretta. Right away, the names catch the eye: *Gretta,* "pearl"; *Gabriel,* angel of truth in the Koran, and in the Book of Daniel the archangel who will sound his trumpet at the Last Judgment and awaken the dead.

Gabriel is not especially likable, and the story is powered by his shortcomings, a series of trivial gaffes and misjudgments that prepare the reader for what is probably the most harmonious of Joyce's epiphanies.

GABRIEL THE GENEROUS

Throughout, Gabriel puts himself in situations that show his true colors— his selfishness and insecurity—but at the end, he undergoes genuine change, as does Barthelme's Simon in *Paradise.* Joyce manipulates Gabriel in order for the reader to grasp fully the extent of his transformation, which enduringly alters his view of life. Gabriel's vision at the end of the story is a moment of revelation for him and a beginning of generosity. Simon, in *Paradise,* has his moment too, and everyone is better for it.

"The Dead" is divided into four string-quartet-like movements (Joyce had a penchant for chamber music): social hour, dinner, aftermath, and the vision. Each is separated by indeterminate time—two beats, two minutes—with successive segments containing more episodes while covering less time. From the first movement to the third, the scope narrows uniformly.

The first appears to maunder, with its roving camera perspective of diverse individuals—Lily the housemaid, the aunts Misses Kate and Julia and their niece Mary Jane, Miss Ivors, Mr. Browne, Freddy Malins and his mother, and others. The disorder in this section—with singing, dancing, conversing, and, of course, drinking—reflects Gabriel's mind, his inability to assimilate all of this.

And there is the matter of his physical appearance: he, like "Stately, plump Buck Mulligan" at the opening of *Ulysses*, is "a stout, tallish young man."

> The high colour of his cheeks pushed upwards even to his fore-head, where it scattered itself in a few formless patches of pale red; and on his hairless face there scintillated restlessly the polished lenses and the bright gilt rims of the glasses which screened his delicate and restless eyes. (Joyce 144)

This is a well-wrought description, and its underlying structure apprises the reader that there is more to this man's vulnerability than skin discoloration, that he attempts, consciously or otherwise, to conceal his liabilities. Joyce heaps on contrarieties in Gabriel, as seen when he tries to make small talk with the maid: "I suppose we'll be going to your wedding one of these fine days with your young man, eh?" Her reply tells him that he's stepped where he should not: "The men that is now is only all palaver and what they can get out of you" (144). It's too much for Gabriel, this bitterness from her suffering, and instead of attempting to comfort her, as he should do, he tries to make it go away with a proffered coin. This is inappropriate behavior. He's unstable, feeling intellectually and socially superior one moment and so perturbed the next that he overreacts to the most innocent actions of others. Or misjudges them. One example of his arrogance shifting to fear is when he's reviewing the talking points for his dinner speech and wonders if lines from Robert Browning will be over the heads of the guests.

> He would only make himself ridiculous by quoting poetry to them which they could not understand. They would think that he was airing his superior education. He would fail with them just as he had failed with the girl in the pantry. He had taken up a wrong tone. His whole speech was a mistake from first to last, an utter failure. (145)

As the story progresses, his separation from the other guests widens. His view of his aunts further puts off the reader. He sees them as "plainly dressed old women," one with a "large flaccid face" whose "slow eyes and parted lips gave her the appearance of a woman who did not know where she was or where she was going," the other "more vivacious" but "all puckers and creases" (145). Later, he thinks of them as "two ignorant old women" (156).

One of his aunts sends him to evaluate the condition of tippler Freddy Malins, who at that moment is telling a rambling story. Gabriel's report is anything but generous, for he tells her that Freddy's state is "hardly noticeable" (150). Gabriel's low self-esteem drives him to tattle, and every time he does it he adds to his burden. Later, he refers to himself "acting as a pennyboy for his aunts" (179).

In the hotel room, Gretta is distant, almost indifferent to him. His frustration increases. "He longed to be master of her strange mood" (177). She is distracted because of something that happened at the party, her reaction to a song being sung as the guests were leaving. The music is painful for her, because it summons the memory of a person she knew long ago; and as Gabriel begins making tentative advances in the hotel room, she makes this known to him. She breaks away and collapses on the bed, hiding her face, just as he, moving toward her, catches his reflection in a mirror and imprints in memory what he sees as a loathsome image.

She tells her story of young, delicate Michael Furey, only 17, who used to sing the same song she heard at the party. Gabriel is initially angry, then bewildered, and remorseful. When he expresses jealousy, she informs him that Furey is long dead.

> Gabriel felt humiliated by the failure of his irony and by the evocation of this figure from the dead, a boy in the gasworks. While he had been full of memories of their secret life together, full of tenderness and joy and desire, she had been comparing him with another. A shameful consciousness of his own person assailed

him. He saw himself as a ludicrous figure, acting as a pennyboy for his aunts, a nervous, well-meaning sentimentalist, orating to vulgarians and idealising his own clownish lusts, the pitiable fatuous fellow he had caught a glimpse of in the mirror. Instinctively he turned his back more to the light lest she might see the shame that burned upon his forehead. (179)

The question Gabriel asks next is inevitable. And it's not without compassion:

"I suppose you were in love with this Michael Furey, Gretta," he said.
"I was great with him at that time," she said.
Her voice was veiled and sad. Gabriel, feeling now how vain it would be to try to lead her whither he had purposed, caressed one of her hands and said, also sadly:
"And what did he die of so young, Gretta? Consumption, was it?"
"I think he died for me," she answered.
A vague terror seized Gabriel at this answer, as if, at that hour when he had hoped to triumph, some impalpable and vindictive being was coming against him, gathering forces against him in its vague world. But he shook himself free of it with an effort of reason and continued to caress her hand. (179)

With Gretta's explanation, Joyce's story rises to its peak of intensity and reaches it with her words: "O, the day I heard that, that he was dead!" (180).

Gabriel, silently and unnoticed by Gretta, withdraws to the window. There is a break in time, long enough for Gretta to fall asleep, and this is when the reader becomes sufficiently close to Gabriel to forgive him for every bad thing he has done on this night.

For the first time, he has discovered Gretta and understands that she is something other than an extension of himself. He is alone with himself, but growing in self-knowledge.

At the beginning of the story, the role of the snow is that of a sinister force, while toward the middle it becomes a means of escape as a vexed Gabriel retreats to the embrasure of a window where he looks out and wishes for release.

In the paragraph that ends the story, the snow serves as a means to measure time—absolute time because what we call real time has ceased.

The snow also is essential to Gabriel's vision. The story's focus, which has narrowed successively through three movements down to Gretta, broadens in the closing two paragraphs. He has turned from looking only within himself first to Gretta and then to the whole of humanity.

> Generous tears filled Gabriel's eyes. He had never felt like that himself towards any woman but he knew that such a feeling must be love. The tears gathered more thickly in his eyes and in the partial darkness he imagined he saw the form of a young man standing under a dripping tree. Other forms were near. His soul had approached that region where dwell the vast hosts of the dead. He was conscious of, but could not apprehend, their wayward and flickering existence. His own identity was facing out into a grey impalpable world: the solid world itself, which these dead had one time reared and lived in, was dissolving and dwindling.
> A few light taps upon the pane made him turn to the window. It had begun to snow again. He watched sleepily the flakes, silver and dark, falling obliquely against the lamplight. The time had come for him to set out on his journey westward. Yes, the newspapers were right: snow was general all over Ireland. It was falling on every part of the dark central plain, on the treeless hills, falling softly upon the Bog of Allen and, farther westward, softly falling into the dark mutinous Shannon waves. It was falling, too, upon every part of the lonely churchyard on the hill where Michael Furey lay buried. It lay thickly drifted on the crooked crosses and headstones, on the spears of the little gate, on the barren thorns. His soul swooned slowly as he heard the snow falling faintly through the universe and faintly falling, like the descent of their last end, upon all the living and the dead. (182)

Joyce, near the end of his life and tormented with self-doubt, alcoholism, and frustration over all his work after *Dubliners* and *A Portrait of the Artist as a Young Man*, declared that the finest short story ever written was Tolstoy's late, simple little fable, "How Much Land Does a Man Need?" This should not be taken seriously, according to John Champlin Gardner, who calls "The Dead" Joyce's finest work (123). Annie Dillard characterizes the story as "seamless" and that its perfection "resides in the total disappearance of ideas into their materials." Joyce's sentences, she goes on, "have in their rhythms an austerity that is complete. They exhibit, by their perfect concealment of it, an absolutely controlled tension, like that of a mastered grief or longing" (161). What about his later work? Certainly, there is even greater craftsmanship and control, but is the work compromised by his artistic choices? The accessibility of *Ulysses* increases with each reading, but the same cannot be said of the *Wake*. In terms of layering, the *Wake* and "The Dead" are at opposite poles. Layers must be peeled back.

THE WEFT OF THE *WAKE*

Finnegans Wake, Donald Barthelme states in a 1963 essay, is a presence that is "always *there,* like the landscape surrounding the reader's home . . . " (13).

A seemly word for the *Wake*—landscape—from the Dutch *landschap,* meaning "region, tract of land." It was in the early 16th century (OED) when the word gained its artistic sense of a picture depicting scenery on land, an expansion brought about by Dutch painters who were just then becoming masters of the genre. Maybe Barthelme wanted it both ways: the *Wake* landscape as a region and as an assemblage.

He knew of Campbell and Robinson's 1944 book *A Skeleton Key to Finnegans Wake*; and some of their statements appear to serve as a starting point for particular arguments in his 1963 commentary "After Joyce."[7] While he would likely take exception to the statement by Campbell and Robinson that the *Wake* is a "mighty allegory of the fall and resurrection of mankind" (13)—arguing that it is more parody than allegory—"After Joyce" reflects accord with their position that the work is "a huge time-capsule, a complete and permanent record of our age" that is "above all else an essay in permanence" (8). Early in their book Campbell and Robinson characterize it as "a kind of terminal moraine in which lie

---

[7] The essay first appeared in *Location,* started in 1963 by Rosenberg, Hess, and Barthelme, and devoted to the arts and literature, and was reprinted in the Spring 1993 *Mississippi Review,* edited by the novelist Frederick Barthelme. *Location* lasted only two issues.

buried all the myths, programmes, slogans, hopes, prayers, tools, educational theories, and the theological bric-á-brac of the past millennium" (8); but conclude that "The complexity of Joyce's imagery results from his titanic fusion of all mythologies," and that the *Wake* "is fellow to the Puranas of the Hindus, the Egyptian Book of the Dead, the Apocalyptic writings of the Persians and the Jews, the scaldic Poetic Edda, and the mystical constructions of the Master singers of the ancient Celts" (294).

The Postmodernist writer would be on friendly territory. In the hallucinatory landscapes of Humphrey Chimpden Earwicker—and Leopold Bloom—Barthelme feels right at home: "Joyce's books present first of all a linguistically exciting surface, dense, glittering, here opaque, here transparent" ("After Joyce" 14). For Barthelme, the *Wake* was collage, "what Joyce did in various ways" (McCaffery 37), he said. "The point of collage is that unlike things are stuck together to make, in the best case, a new reality. This new reality, in the best case, may be or imply a comment on the other reality from which it came, and may be also much else. It's an *itself,* if it's successful . . ." (Klinkowitz 51–52).

True to Postmodernist principles, Barthelme insists in "After Joyce" that a work like the *Wake* "is not about something but *is* something . . . an object in the world rather than a text or commentary upon the world." Joyce, he points out, was seeing this in the painting of his own time (13), first in the Constructivism movement, then in Cubism, Dadaism, and Surrealism. He took more than a passing interest in the work of Marcel Duchamp (Theall 2), particularly in French Dadaist images depicting sequential movements of a body (*American Academic*).

Being an *itself* raises a major issue, the nature of the literary object. Barthelme explores this in the essay:

> Interrogating older works, the question is: what do they say about the world and being in the world? But the literary object is itself "world" and the theoretical advantage is that in asking it questions you are asking questions of the world directly. This sounds like a species of ventriloquism—the writer throwing his voice. But it is,

rather, a stunning strategic gain for the writer. He has in fact
removed himself from the work, just as Joyce instructed him to do.
The reader is not listening to an authoritative account of the world
delivered by an expert (Faulkner on Mississippi, Hemingway on
the corrida) but bumping into something that is *there*, like a rock or
a refrigerator. (13)

The reader, he explains, becomes

a voyager in the world coming upon a strange object. The reader
reconstitutes the work by his active participation, by approaching
the object, tapping it, shaking it, holding it to his ear to hear the
roaring within. It is characteristic of the object that it does not
declare itself all at once, in a rush of pleasant naïveté. (14)

As stated earlier, Barthelme had changed his mind by the mid-80s as to the
literary object's relationship to the world. He was, he admits, "beguiled by the
rhetoric of the time," but even in the 1980s, the "proposition's still attractive"
(123).

A couple of years ago I visited Willem de Kooning's studio in East
Hampton, and when the big doors are opened one can't help
seeing—it's a shock—the relation between the rushing green world
outside and the paintings. Precisely how de Kooning manages to
distill nature into art is a mystery, but the explosive relation is
there, I've seen it. Once when I was in Elaine de Kooning's studio
on Broadway, at a time when the metal sculptor Herbert Ferber
occupied the studio immediately above, there came through the
floor a most horrible crashing and banging. "What in the world is
that?" I asked, and Elaine said, "Oh, that's Herbert thinking." (123)

And here he clarifies his modified position on the art object in the world:

Art is a true account of the activity of the mind. Because
consciousness, in Husserl's formulation, is always consciousness
of something, art thinks ever of the world, cannot not think of the
world, could not turn its back on the world even if it wished to.
This does not mean that it's going to be honest as a mailman; it's
more likely to appear as a drag queen. The problems . . . enforce
complexity. "We do not spend much time in front of a canvas
whose intentions are plain," writes Cioran, "music of a specified
character, unquestionable contours, exhausts our patience, the

over-explicit poem seems . . .   incomprehensible.
("Not-Knowing" 123)

Edmund Husserl,[8] German philosopher and contemporary of Joyce, is the founder of phenomenology and who contended that consciousness has no life apart from the objects it contemplates. Barthelme, in the 1971 interview admits to having "taken a certain degree of nourishment (or stolen a lot) from the phenomenologists: Sartre, Erwin Straus" (Klinkowitz 52); and in "Not-Knowing" he pokes fun at Existentialism, "which I never thought was anything more than Phenomenology's bathwater anyway" (115). Husserl's later work was in idealism, George Berkeley's doctrine denying that objects exist outside of consciousness. Berkeley[9] was well known to Joyce, a great admirer of idealist writer William Blake on whom he lectured in 1912 as he was about to begin *Ulysses*. One statement Joyce made in this talk stands out: "Blake killed the dragon of experience and natural wisdom, and, by minimizing space and time and denying the existence of memory and the senses, he tried to paint his works on the void of the divine bosom" (Ellmann, *Ulysses on the Liffey* 15).

HARDWARE AND SOFTWARE

Joyce, he says—and Barthelme could be talking about himself—"proceeds like a man weaving a blanket of what might be found in a hardware store. The strangeness of his project is an essential part of it, almost its point. The fabric falls apart, certainly, but where it hangs together we are privileged to encounter a world made new. . ." ("After Joyce" 14).

Not only the hardware store, but the public house, the newspaper, the magazine, the broadcast, film, medicine, Freud, sex—it's all there, woven into the Joycean blanket.

---

[8] Husserl, 1859-1938.

[9] Berkeley, 1685-1753.

Technology attracted him too, at a time when he was developing as an artist. When he began working on the *Wake* in 1922, mechanization, electricity and electrification were part of everyday life, and between the first and second World Wars, European art and letters, including music, architecture, and dance, became almost obsessed with the possibilities of new technologies (Theall 2).

In the 50-year span before his birth, the industrialized world witnessed the development of the telegraph, the telephone, the camera, the typewriter, the high-speed rotary press and the power generator.

Between 1877 and the year Joyce was born, 1882, Edison patented the carbon microphone, the record player, and the incandescent lamp. During Joyce's boyhood the Eiffel tower went up; the first execution by electrocution was carried out; and the Lumière brothers patented and demonstrated the first documented machines for photographing, printing, and projecting film. Pierre and Marie Curie discovered radium; Marconi received the first transatlantic radio transmission; the Wright brothers flew the first heavier-than-air, mechanically propelled airplane; and people flocked to see the 12-minute silent film *The Great Train Robbery*. As Einstein formulated the General Theory of Relativity, Ford adapted the assembly line to automobile manufacture (*Academic American*).

It was almost inevitable then, given Joyce's predilections, that the machines and implications of science and technology, along with the tools of everyday communication, would find their way into the *Wake*.

Especially the *Wake*. Theall points out that "the new modes of popular culture and electrified mechanization held a particular attraction for an author reconstructing the night of an 'Everybody' (HCE), for the dream action which takes place that night also retraces the social evolution of technology" (4).

The promise perceived by many motivated them to recreate themselves. Theall attaches some importance to the line, "First you were Nomad, next you were Namar, now you're Numah and it's soon you'll be Nomon" (*FW* 374.22), believing it to reveal the record of "the people" making themselves over: *Nomad* being wanderers, *Namar* warriors, *Numah* the alienated, and *Nomon* those like Odysseus who would transcend human limits (4). McHugh deciphers *nomon* as "no more" (374), while Theall favors "no one," calling Joyce's construction "a complex pun probably involving elements such as: nomos + gnomon + noman, i.e., law & custom + one who interprets or knows + no man + know man + *Ulysses*' name = no one" (4).

Throughout the long night of the *Wake* and particularly in the latter part of it, references appear to cinema, radio, newspapers, "dupenny" magazines, comics—Thimble Theatre (from the Popeye series), Little Orphan Annie, Moon Mullins, and Shirley Temple's *Wee Willie Winkie* (Theall 11).

The *tele-* prefix materializes frequently: there's *teleframe, telekinesis, telemac, telepath, telephone, telephony, telescope, telesmell, telesphorously, televisible, television, televox, telewisher.* Also encountered are *velivision* and *dullaphone* (Theall 4–5).

The rational reader eventually asks, what's the point? In letters to Harriet Shaw Weaver during the composition of the *Wake*, Joyce half-jokingly says that he sees himself as an engineer and goes on to describe his project:

> I am making an engine with only one wheel. No spokes of course. The wheel is a perfect square. You see what I am driving at, don't you? I am awfully solemn about it, mind you, so you must not think of it as a silly story about the mookse and the grapes. No, it's a wheel, I tell the world. *And* it's all *square.* (*Letters* 251)

Ellmann explains that he means "the book ended where it began, like a wheel, that it had four books or parts, like the four sides of a square, and that *Finnegans Wake* contained the *doubles entendres* of a wake (funeral) and wake (awakening or resurrection), as well as of Fin (end) and again (recurrence)" (*James Joyce* 609).

This four-part cycle, of course, Joyce derived from 18th-century philosopher Giambattista Vico. In *La Scienza Nuova,* Vico contends that history passes through four phases: theocratic, aristocratic, democratic and chaotic. The final phase is distinguished, as Joyce views his own time, by self-indulgence, self-absorption, and sterility. It is the bottom of man's fall (Campbell and Robinson 14).

This poetic engineer concept manifested itself in artistic sensibility from 1905 until the end of the Second World War, as Joyce and many other writers and artists of the time pondered every new development in science and technology. Joyce's friend Paul Valéry maintained that engineering methods and poetic methods were essentially the same, an idea that goes back to Renaissance poetics and is also sanctioned by Vico (Theall 6).

The *Wake* reflects discoveries being made at the time by Joyce, shaping and reshaping his book to make it conform to a changing world. The *Wake* was a machine, and he was the engineer whose task it was to incorporate all applicable developments in science and technology.

He gave a great deal of thought to arts and communication of the period, and tried to project where they might end up. Theall says, "Joyce realized how extensively these activities involved new modes of social organization and of technological production, reproduction and distribution that insisted on the exploration of the relation of all poetic communication to the 'machinic.'" This term goes beyond *mechanical*.

Machinic "calls attention to the fact that all machinery is first and foremost socially grounded," Theall says, and that poetic communication like the "'machinic' is an assemblage which is social before being technical" (7).

Even so, mechanics, chemistry, and mathematics power the engine of *Finnegans Wake*, and its very structure, Joyce insists, is mathematical (3). Numerical references begin early in early in the text, in the fifth paragraph. The building mentioned in this lengthy passage, "a waalworth of a skyerscape of most eyeful hoyth entowerly" (*FW* 4:35), is identified by McHugh as the 60-story Woolworth skyscraper at 233 Broadway in New York City, completed in 1913. In

60

the paragraph, the altitude of the edifice is being calculated by Finnegan the hod carrier[10]

> Bygmester Finnegan . . . with goodly trowel in grasp and ivoroiled overalls which he habitacularly fondseed, like Haroun Childeric Eggeberth he would caligulate by multiplicables the alltitude and malltitude (*FW* 4.18–33)

In the Triv and Quad section, along with humor, language—including some good-natured parody of old rhetorical theory—and the arts of the trivium, Joyce treats language as a mathematical structure and an engineering problem as children learn geometry, algebra, combinations, permutations and probabilities (Theall 9).

Putting aside for a moment that the *Wake* is written in code, Joyce makes several references to code itself, to telegraphy, with "this new book of Morses" (*FW* 123.35)—and to Moses, writing the Pentateuch (McHugh). Telegraphy is yet another in the series of "mechanics" that Theall maintains "are important for the *Wake*, since they represent the moment when the mechanical is electrified." The electric media, the telegraph, is a continuation of the early manuscript—"a transformation of the potentialities" of it, in Theall's words, "just as the manuscript is of the 'wordcraft' of 'woodwordings'" (14).

Joyce alludes to photochemistry:

> Well, almost any photoist worth his chemicots will tip anyone asking him the teaser that if a negative of a horse happens to melt while drying, well, what you do get is, well, a positively grotesquely distorted micromass of all sorts of horsehappy values and masses of meltwhile horse. Tip. (*FW* 111.27)

---

[10] Campbell and Robinson: "Tim Finnegan of the old Vaudeville song is an Irish hod carrier who gets drunk, falls off a ladder, and is apparently killed. His friends hold a deathwatch over his coffin; during the festivities someone splashes him with whiskey, at which Finnegan comes to life again and joins in the general dance. On this comedy-song foundation, Joyce bases the title of his work. But there is more, much more, to the story. Finnegan the hod carrier is identifiable first with Finn MacCool, captain for two hundred years of Ireland's warrior-heroes, and most famous of Dublin's early giants. Finn typifies *all* heroes—Thor, Prometheus, Osiris, Christ, the Buddha—in whose life and through whose inspiration the race lives. It is by Finn's coming again (Finnagain)—in other words, by the reappearance of the hero—that strength and hope are provided for mankind" (14).

He brings up electrolysis with the use of the word *helixtrolysis* in a discussion about dairy machinery (*FW* 163.31) (McHugh).

Several times, he mentions the cinema, early on in a digression during the investigation of HCE's alleged transgression in the park. "And roll away the reel world, the reel world, the reel world!" (*FW* 64.25)—which is to say, roll the film. "Now for a strawberry frolic!" (64.26). A reference follows to American film star Noah Beery (64.32).

Joyce's admiration of the cinema is evident in the *Wake*. In 1929 he met an individual who would become one of the top film directors of all time, Sergei Eisenstein. He had been aware of Joyce's work for at least a year. In a monograph for the *Cinéma d'Ajourd'hui* series, Eisenstein confidant Léon Moussinac includes a 1928 letter he received from the Russian filmmaker asking about Joyce:

> As always, I have a favor to ask. It's just that I still have one main passion: James Joyce. His new work is being published in Paris right now, in the journal *Transition*. The favor is to get   me   a subscription and send me the issues containing Joyce's new novel *Finnegans Wake*. It seems to me that little by little Joyce is becoming more and more "à la mode." There must be a lot of things coming out about him. . . . What Joyce does with literature is quite close to what we're trying to do with the new cinematography, and even closer to what we're going to do. . . . (Moussinac 147–48)

When they met the following year, the impression Joyce made on Eisenstein as they talked about filming *Ulysses* must have been powerful, for Moussinac writes:

> The montage possibilities of the "internal monologue" of Joyce's Leopold Bloom had long occupied the imagination of Eisenstein, for, as he later expressed it, he was fascinated by the process of listening to "one's own train of thought, particularly in an excited state, in order to catch yourself looking at and listening to your mind. . . . In Joyce, Eisenstein found a man to whom his aims and methods were intelligible. They talked of the future development of their mutual preoccupation—the "internal monologue"—how the processes of the mind could be made visible and

comprehensible through the film medium. Despite his near-blindness, Joyce wanted to see those sections of *Potemkin* and *October*, [also known as] *Ten Days That Shook the World* in which [Eisenstein] had tried to reveal the inner core of man and, thus, convey reality to the spectator. (Moussinac 39–40)

Whether Joyce ever got around to seeing *Battleship Potemkin*[11] or *October*[12] is not reported, but Moussinac does relate Joyce saying that he wanted Eisenstein to direct *Ulysses* if ever it was filmed. Eisenstein is quoted telling associates: "Joyce alone among living writers was breaking down the walls of literary tradition and creating new forms to express the inner process of thought and emotion" (39).

Cinematic and television references appear in the beginning of Book II of the *Wake* (219.8). A play given by children for their parents in Feenichts (Phoenix) Playhouse, "with the benediction of the Holy Genesius Archimachus [God] (219.8) is to be "wordloosed over seven seas crowdblast in cellelle-neteutoslavzendlatinsoundscript. In four tubbloids" (219.16). In addition there are "Shadows by the film folk" (221.21) with "Longshots, upcloses, outblacks and stagetolets" (221.23), and "Melodiotiosities in purefusion by the score" (222.2). There is interwoven media here as well: Joyce has a stage performance being filmed and televised over short wave.

Following the Triv and Quad section comes a series of scenes in Earwicker's establishment, the Tavernry in Feast chapter. The 12 customers—"Overtones of the Last Supper are certainly present" (Campbell and Robinson 164)—have taken up a collection and purchased for HCE a

> tolvtubular high fidelity daildialler, as modern as tomorrow afternoon and in appearance up to the minute . . . equipped with supershielded umbrella antennas for distance getting and connected by the magnetic links of a Bellini-Tosti coupling system with a vitaltone speaker, capable of capturing skybuddies, harbour craft emittences, key clickings, viaticum cleaners, due to woman formed mobile or man made static and bawling the whowle hamshack and wobble down in an eliminium sounds pound so as to

---

[11] 1925
[12] 1927

> serve him up a melegoturny marygoraumd, eclectrically filtered for
> allirish earths and ohmes. This harmonic condenser enginium (the
> Mole) they   caused to be worked from a magazine battery. . . .
> (309.14–310.2).

This is a tongue-in-cheek passage and it serves an unintended purpose: like Toto
in Oz, it pulls back the curtain and shows Barthelme's hardware-store blanket-
weaving wizard at work. And *where* he is while he works—not in a hardware
store but a public house

The *dialdialler* reference is to a popular short-wave receiver of the 1930s,
the Sky Buddy, manufactured by the Hallicrafters Company of Chicago and a
popular item on the shelf behind the bar. Earwicker's radio is "capable of
capturing skybuddies," or sky bodies (McHugh), and just about everything else, it
would seem. Sky Buddies were six-tube radios, not "tolvtubular"(a 12-tube
model—Joyce must have come across that device in an ad), but were advertised
as having good tone, "high fidelity," and could be powered from a battery.
"Supershielded umbrella antennas" might refer to imposing arrays used by coastal
land stations that handled communications with ships at sea, but many publicans
of the time would have had a simpler two-wire version of an "umbrella" on the
roof of their establishments to monitor short wave broadcasts and "harbor craft
emmittences." Patrons of a seacoast pub might listen to local harbor
communications for entertainment, especially for the salty language of mariners.
Much radio reception in these times would be accompanied by a cacophony of
"key clickings," interference from nearby coastal land stations transmitting
telegraphy, which could be heard on most listening apparatus in a two- or three-
mile radius. However, the vacuum cleaner, another source of everyday
interference, is more layering of that which glitters: "vaticum" suggests Vatican
Radio, which Irish denizens of a drinking establishment might monitor while
imbibing, and also evokes, according to McHugh, *viaticum*—the Eucharist.
Therefore, the "cleaner," the purification.

Joyce at work, troweling one glittering layer over another.

Sound from this wondrous radio is routed to "a meatous conch" (310.12), a horn for the auditory canal (meatus), something like headphones, that could bring to HCE anything he might want to hear—Campbell and Robinson specify "all broadcasts, so as to lull [him]" (165)—until the end of his "otological life" (310.21).

Campbell and Robinson use the word *televisioning* (164) to characterize what is occurring in certain sections of this chapter. Joyce himself seems to have been doing a bit of televisioning, as indicated by details of television technology that he has incorporated in the TV episode of the vaudevillian brothers Butt and Taff:

> Sing in the chorias to the ethur:
> [*In the heliotropical noughttime following a fade of transformed Tuff and, pending its viseversion, a metenergic reglow of beaming Batt, the bairdboard bombardment screen, if tastefully taut guranium satin, tends to teleframe and step up tothe charge of a light barricade. Down the photoslope in syncopanc pulses, with the bitts bugtwug their teffs, the missledhropes, glitteraglatteraglutt, borne by their carnier walve. Spraygun rakes and splits them from a double focus: grenadite, damnymite, alextronite, nichilite: and the scanning firespot of the sgunners traverses the rutilanced illustred sunksundered lines. Shlossh! . . .*] (349.6 ff.)

The word "ethur" can be "aether" (McHugh 349), the clear upper air breathed by the Olympians, as well as "ether," once believed to be the medium of propagation for electromagnetic waves. Taff and Butt are transformed by the medium— "viceversion" or vice versa—to Tuff and Batt. John Logie Baird invented television and in 1926 successfully transmitted a 30-line image of a face. In 1928 this Scot demonstrated color TV and announced his invention of the Phonodisc, the first video disc system (*Academic American*). "Bairdboard" is a play on "breadboard," a prototype of an electrical device, Baird's version generating electrons and bombarding the TV screen with them.

In the next line, "guranium" is uranium, suggesting the brilliant red of a geranium, and "teleframe" is one complete scan of the TV screen;

"step up" refers to amplification of the charge of light, with "barricade" making it a play on *The Charge of the Light Brigade.*

"Photoslope" is the path taken by the synchronizing—"syncopanc"— pulses of the TV signal, transporting the "missledhropes," Irish missile troops, with bits between their teeth, on a carrier wave (all McHugh). The allusion to a bit in a horse's mouth is obvious, of course, but these entities are transporting information as well. Based on this and other references in the *Wake*, Joyce apparently must have known of the concept of the bit as a unit of information. The idea originated with physicist Leo Szilard, who had come up with the idea in 1920 while studying for his doctorate at the University of Berlin (Dannen 90). The "spraygun" is the electron gun that focuses the information on the scanning spot of the "sunksundered lines," that is, the 600-line screen. "Shlossh" is German *Schluss*, the end.

The *Wake* is a dream, of course, and Theall believes that Earwicker and Anna Livia Plurabelle make up the body of the dreamer. "Their conjunction (wedding and marriage) —'from a bride's eye stammpunct when a man that means a mountain . . . wades a lymph' (*FW* 309.4)—quite literally plays on the two-in-one theme, the biblical motif used in the Catholic Marriage ceremony of two-in-one-flesh" (Theall 24). The narrative is sometimes a mingling and other times a coalescing of their voices.

Anna Livia, according to Campbell and Robinson, is "a river, always changing yet ever the same, the Heraclitean flux which bears all life on its current. . . . She is the circular river of time, flowing past Eve and Adam in the first sentence of the book, bearing in her flood the debris of dead civilizations and the seeds of crops and cultures yet to come." Her cycle "is a perfect example of the Viconian *corso* and *recorso*—the circular ground-plan on which *Finnegans Wake* is laid" (18–19). "Men, cities, empires, and whole systems bubble and burst in her river of time. . . . All of the contending parties . . . are mothered and cherished by her. Them she affirms as she slips between the river banks on her dream journey to the sea of renewal" (297).

She is energy. She carries one charge and Earwicker another. There is attraction and repulsion, "polar energies that spin the universe," explain Campbell and Robinson. "Wherever Joyce looks in history or human life, he discovers the operation of these basic polarities. . . . Amid trivia and tumult, by prodigious symbol and mystic sign . . . Joyce presents, develops, amplifies and recondenses nothing more nor less than the eternal dynamic implicit in birth, conflict, death, and resurrection" (21).

THE LAY OF THE LANDSCAPE

Among other things, Joyce was trying to project where the technology of his time might lead. Theall's premise for Joyce's rationale:

> Imagine Joyce around 1930 asking the question: what is the role of the book in a culture which has discovered photography, phonography, radio, film, television, telegraph, cable, and telephone and has developed newspapers, magazines, advertising, Hollywood, and sales promotion? What people read, they will now go to see in film and on television; everyday life will appear in greater detail and more up-to-date fashion in the press, on radio and in television; oral poetry will be reanimated by the potentialities of sound recording. (11)

Similarly, for Barthelme, "[t]he artist's effort, always and everywhere, is to attain a fresh mode of cognition," and to achieve this he must distance himself from the commonplace. "What makes the literary object a work of art is the intention of the artist." He offers as example the American painter Roy Lichtenstein, who when he "proposes as art a blown-up comic strip, a replica in every detail except in scale of an actual comic strip, we are presented with the artist's intention, his gesture, in its nakedness." Barthelme suggests that Lichtenstein's "statement" might be a question: *"What do you think of a society in which these things are seen as art?"* Thus, "social and historical concerns re-enter the ambience of the work. Far from implying a literature that is its own subject matter, the work that is an object is rich in possibilities" and the artist "has placed himself in a position to gain access to a range of meanings previously inaccessible to his art." Joyce, he says, is one of the few who have used such a strategy, and "the reasons for this are obvious. Not only have there been highly visible failures, but even the successes have been intimidating. *Finnegans Wake* is not a work which encourages emulation" ("After Joyce" 14).

He mentions Ezra Pound's reaction at some stage of his reading of the *Wake*: "I will have another go at it, but up to present I make nothing of it whatever. Nothing so far as I make out, nothing short of divine vision or a new cure for the clapp can possibly be worth all that circumambient peripherization" (Ellmann, *James Joyce* 597).

This, Barthelme says, "has remained the general (if covert) opinion. Writers borrow Joyce's myth-patterning or stream-of-consciousness and regard *Wake* as a monument or an obsession, in any case something that does not have to be repeated. ("After Joyce" 14)

Some might take the appraisal of Joyce's brother Stanislaus as a compliment: "You have done the longest day in literature, and now you are conjuring up the deepest night" (Ellmann 591).

But not that of Nora Barnacle: "Why don't you write sensible books that people can understand?" (Ellmann 603).

In a rare defense of his work Joyce says, "One great part of every human existence is passed in a state which cannot be rendered sensible by the use of wideawake language, cutanddry grammar and goahead plot" (Ellmann 597). Barthelme echoes this in his statement "[W]e are looking for the as-yet unspeakable, the as-yet unspoken" ("Not-Knowing" 117),

Campbell and Robinson state that Joyce never subscribed "to the journalistic fallacy that everything should be made easy to understand. He knew that there are levels of experience and consciousness that can be reached only by a prodigious effort of the part of the creative artist, and comprehended only after a comparable effort on the part of the audience." They cite Nietzsche's version of his own creative struggle: "I write in blood, I will be read in blood." This, they say, "is applicable tenfold to Joyce [whose] youth had been nurtured on such sacramental fare that he was nauseated by the sweetish, sawdust loaf offered to the populace as true bread" (295).

The *Wake* and creations like it, Barthelme observes in "After Joyce," have the power to change the beholder: "I do not think it fanciful, for instance, to say that Governor [Nelson] Rockefeller, standing among his Miros and de Koonings, is worked upon by them, and if they do not make a Democrat or a Socialist of him they at least alter the character of his Republicanism" (14).

Or for that matter, anyone's *-ism*. Prominent in Barthelme's consciousness in 1963 when he was writing "After Joyce" was the USSR with its aura of invincibility, and his observations on threats to systems and to ways of life are valid today:

> Soviet hostility to "formalist" art becomes more intelligible, as does the antipathy of senators, mayors and chairmen of building committees. In the same way, Joyce's book works its radicalizing will upon all men in all countries, even upon those who have not read it and will never read it. (14)

WORKS CITED IN THE CHAPTER

Academic American Encyclopedia. Grolier Multimedia Encyclopedia Version (V 8.10). Danbury: Grolier Electronic Publishing, 1996.

Barth, John. *Further Fridays: Essays, Lectures, and Other Nonfiction 1984–94.* Boston: Little Brown, 1995.

Barthelme, Donald. "After Joyce." *Location.* New York: Longview Foundation, 1963. 13–16.

——. "Not-Knowing." *Major Writers of Short Fiction.* Ann Charters, ed. Boston: Bedford Books of St. Martin's P, 1993. 113–24.

Campbell, Joseph, and Henry Morton Robinson. *A Skeleton Key to Finnegans Wake.* 1944. Cutchogue, New York: Buccaneer Books, 1976.

Dannen, Gene. "The Einstein-Szilard Refrigerators." *Scientific American.* January 1997: 90–95.

Dillard, Annie. *Living by Fiction.* New York: Harper & Row, 1988.

Eco, Umberto. "Postmodernism, Irony, the Enjoyable." *Postscript to* The Name of the Rose. San Diego: Harcourt Brace Jovanovich, 1984.

Ellmann, Richard. *James Joyce.* New York: Oxford U P, 1959.

——. *Ulysses on the Liffey.* New York: Oxford U P, 1972.

Gardner, John. *The Art of Fiction.* New York: Knopf, 1984.

Gass, William H. *Fiction and the Figures of Life.* Boston: David R. Godine, 1989.

Joyce, James "The Dead." *Dubliners.* New York: Bantam, 1990. 142–82.

——. *Finnegans Wake.* New York: Penguin, 1976.

Klinkowitz, Jerome. "Donald Barthelme." *The New Fiction: Interviews with Innovative American Writers*. Ed. Joe David Bellamy. Urbana: U of Illinois P, 1974. 45–54.

Letters: James Joyce to Harriet Shaw Weaver. Stuart Gilbert, ed. New York: Viking, 1957.

McCaffery, Larry. "An Interview with Donald Barthelme." *Anything Can Happen: Interviews with Contemporary American Novelists.* Ed. Thomas LeClair and McCaffery. Urbana: U of Illinois P, 1983. 32–44.

McHugh, Roland. *Annotations to Finnegans Wake.* Baltimore: Johns Hopkins U P, 1991.

Moussinac, Léon. *Sergei Eisenstein: An investigation into his films and philosophy.* New York: Crown, 1970.

Newman, Charles. *The Post-Modern Aura: The Act of Fiction in an Age of Inflation.* Evanston: Northwestern U P, 1985.

Theall, Donald F. "The Hieroglyphs of Engined Egypsians: Machines, Media and Modes of Communication in *Finnegans Wake.*" *Joyce Studies Annual.* Thomas F. Staley, ed. Austin: U of Texas P, 1991. 129–76.

4 FIRST NOVEL: *SNOW WHITE*

In a questionnaire placed close to the center of his 1967 *Snow White*, Barthelme asks the reader: "Do you like the story so far?" and "Has the work, for you, a metaphysical dimension?" He goes on: "Is there too much *blague* in the narration? Not enough *blague?"* (Barthelme 82–83).

Blague is pretentious falsehood, humbug (OED), the latter term, of course, covering *hoax, impostor, nonsense,* and *pretense*. His own answer regarding *blague* is apparent in the 1981 O'Hara interview: "I think that in this book the prose is far too worked, wrought, banged upon, too many jokes—a nervousness on my part that shouldn't be there. I don't regret having published it or anything of that sort, but it could have been better." (O'Hara 205). A year later, his position remains unchanged: "It's not my favorite book" (Brans 124).

John Barth, in his *Times Book Review* eulogy to Barthelme, praises *Snow White*, insisting that "the novel is *blague*-free, like all of Donald Barthelme's writing. Not enough to say he didn't waste words . . . . Donald barely *indulged* words—he valued them too much for that—and this rhetorical short leash makes his occasional lyric flights all the more exhilarating. . ." (9).

Although *Snow White* is a first novel, Barth says the label does not apply here: "Is there really any 'early Donald Barthelme'? Like Mozart and Kafka, he seems to have been born full-grown." Changes that occurred over the decades, Barth contends were merely cosmetic, "some minor lengthening and shortening of his literary sideburns," but "he never forsook what Borges calls 'that element of irrealism indispensable to art'. Later in the piece Barth refers to Barthelme's recognizable figures of popular mythology as an "alloy of irrealism and its opposite" (9).

Snow White opens with what can only be called a map: "She is a tall dark beauty containing a great many beauty spots: one above the breast, one above the belly, one above the knee, one above the ankle, one above the buttock, one on the back of the neck. All of these are on the left side, more or less in a row as you go up and down." What follows are six printer's bullets, set in a straight vertical line that leads to a single sentence: "The hair is black as ebony, the skin white as snow"(3).

As more is revealed about her—she's alternately bored, unpredictable, compulsive, narcissistic, and without "a pinch of emotion coloring the jet black of her jet-black eyes" (10)—a fine tension is set up between what she's supposed to be and what she is here. Certainly, she's physically similar to the Disney version, and to the original *Schneewittchen* in the German tale of the Brothers Grimm collection. What happens in Barthelme's novel is that the *Schneewittchen* becomes the *doppelgänger*, the ghostly double haunting and weaving a spell over her Postmodern counterpart, who knows the old story and the role she's supposed to play. The contrarieties at work here—the impostor, her hoax and pretenses, and the other characters with their consciousness of self and awareness of the story on which they are based, each trying to play the role of their counterpart in the original—generate disharmony and greater tension. And they're all double-minded.

Snow White's first utterance in the novel, the plaint "Oh I wish there were some words in the world that were not the words I always hear!," reverberates throughout the narrative. The seven try to come up with something new, getting off to a bad start with *fish slime* and *injunctions,* but at last achieving a breakthrough: "Murder and create!' Henry said, and that was weak, but we applauded, and Snow White said, 'That is one I've never heard before ever,' and that gave us courage" (6).

As regards the narrative voice associated with the seven, Barthelme explains: "The presence of the seven men made possible a 'we' narration that offered some tactical opportunities—there's a sort of generalized narrator, a group spokesman who could be any one of the seven" (McCaffery 43).

Opportunities also presented themselves in the Snow White mythology, he says. "[T]he usefulness of the Snow White story is that everybody knows it and it can be played against. . . . Every small change in the story is momentous when everybody knows the story backward" (McCaffery 43). The wicked stepmother in the novel is Jane, usually linked with Tarzan but here presented as a compeer of Snow White. Doing this, Barthelme says, "was a way of placing the emphasis on Snow White's network of relationships with the seven cohabitors" (O'Hara 205).

Like the others, Jane looks back to the original. "I was fair once. . . . I was the fairest of them all. Men came from miles around simply to be in my power. But those days are gone. Those better days. Now I cultivate my malice." She's quick to add that it is "not the pale natural malice we knew, when the world was young," that she has grown more witchlike and has invented new varieties of malice, that men have not seen before now" (Barthelme 40).

Friend to Snow White or not, Jane is what she's always been, and now "must witch someone, for that is my role. . . ." While deciding what form her malice should take, she visits the rare-poison pantry of her mother's exclusive duplex apartment, eyeing jars of bane with neatly done labels like *dayshade, scumlock, hurtwort, milkleg.* "Whose interpersonal relations shall I poison, with the tasteful savagery of my abundant imagination and talent for concoction? I think I will go around to Snow White's house, where she cohabits with the seven men in a mocksome travesty of approved behavior, and see what is stirring there." Should something be stirring, she says, "perhaps I can arrange a sleep for it—in the corner of a churchyard, for example" (Barthelme 158).

While Jane comes close to her counterpart, the seven stand in contrast to theirs. Instead of Bashful, Sleepy, Sneezy, Grumpy, Happy, Dopey, and Doc, they are Bill, Kevin, Clem, Hubert, Henry, Edward, and Dan; and they have sex with Snow White, not infrequently in the shower. Except for Bill, that is, who has · grown tired of her (4). The seven, Barthelme insists, are not dwarfs: "They are consistently spoken of as men. Of course that could be read as little men" (Brans 124).

Little in several senses is Snow White's take: "The seven of them only add up to the equivalent of two *real men,* as we know them from the films and from our childhood, when there were giants on the earth. It is possible of course that there are no more *real men* here, on this ball of half-truths, the earth" (Barthelme 41–42).

Seven equals two: according to Barthelme, "this arithmetic is the center of the novel, gives rise to the question of what *real men* are, what the attitudes of the male characters mean" (O'Hara 205).

THE DAYS OF GIANTS

Snow White's reference to the days when giants walked the earth, "from our childhood," is not only to the fairy-tale world but to the childhood of humankind as related in Genesis. The probable source could be Genesis 6, 4: "There were giants in the earth in those days; and also after that, when the sons of God came in unto the daughters of men, and they bare children to them, the same became mighty men which were of old, men of renown" (KJV). The Catholic Biblical Association translation of the same verse refers to them as *Nephilim,* the name the Israelites gave the prehistoric giants of Palestine: "At that time the Nephilim appeared on earth . . . after the sons of heaven had intercourse with the daughters of man, who bore them sons. They were the heroes of old, the men of renown" (New American Bible).

Giants, tall shining knights in quest of the Grail—heroes, real men. Snow White knows what's supposed to happen: the princely rescue. She calls out the name of the book's prince-figure: "Paul? Is there a Paul, or have I only projected him in the shape of my longing, boredom, ennui and pain? Have I been trained in the finest graces and arts all my life for nothing but this?. . . There is a Paul somewhere, but not here. Not under my window. Not yet" (Barthelme 102).

Indeed, there is a Paul, but he is elsewhere, wondering, "'What is the next thing demanded of me by history?'" (Barthelme 55). Postmodern prince that he is, he knows the role too. "'I am princely,'" Paul reflected in his eat-in kitchen. "'There is that. At times, when I am "down," I am able to pump myself up again by thinking about my blood. It is blue, the bluest this fading world has known probably."

Sometimes he frightens himself "'with a gesture so royal, so full of light, that I wonder where it comes from.'" The answer is, from his father, Paul XVII, whose height of ambition "'was to tumble the odd chambermaid now and then, whereas I have loftier ambitions, only I don't know what they are, exactly.'" He knows that the thing to do is "go out and effect a liaison with some beauty who needs me, and save her, and ride away with her flung over the pommel of my palfrey, I believe I have that right. But on the other hand, this duck-with-blue-cheese sandwich that I am eating is mighty attractive and absorbing, too" (Barthelme 27–28).

In his questionnaire, Barthelme asks: "Have you understood, in reading to this point, that Paul is the prince-figure?" (82).

On a page headed *"The psychology of Snow White,"* the question "What does she hope for?" is answered with: "'Someday my prince will come.'" A confused explanation follows: "By this Snow White means that she lives her own being as incomplete, pending the arrival of one who will 'complete' her. That is, she lives her own being as 'not-with' (even though she is in some sense 'with' the seven men . . .). As with the grass in the distant field, "the 'not-with' is experienced as stronger, more real, at this particular instant in time, than the 'being-with.' The incompleteness is an ache capable of subduing all other data presented by consciousness" (70).

As housekeeper—"a horsewife" (43)—to the seven, she cleans compulsively, washing the pans and grates of the gas range, clearing the ports of the gas orifices with a hairpin, rinsing the broiler; then moving on to the books and spraying them for book lice with a five-percent solution of DDT, afterwards oiling the bindings with neat's-foot oil. This done, she begins "piano care" (37–38).

On the following page, set in bold capitals like a chapter title:

WHAT SNOW WHITE REMEMBERS:
THE HUNTSMAN
THE FOREST
THE STEAMING KNIFE (39)

At the top of an otherwise empty page: *"Miseries and complaints of Snow White:* 'I am tired of being just a horsewife!'" (43).

Early in the novel, the seven arrive home to find that Snow White has "written a dirty great poem four pages long, won't let us read it, refuses absolutely" (10). Its nature is the issue: "The poem remained between us like an immense, wrecked railroad car" (59). You haven't heard the last of this, she tells them: "'Like the long-sleeping stock certificate suddenly alive in its green safety-deposit box because of new investor interest, my imagination is stirring. Be warned'" (59–60).

Following, and facing the latter page, are more headings, among them: "The Horsewife in History, Famous Horsewives. . .Views of St. Augustine, Views of the Venerable Bede, Emerson on the American Horsewife, Oxford Companion to the American Horsewife, Introduction of Bon Ami . . .The Plastic Bag, The Garlic Press" (61).

Similar titles appear throughout the novel and function as chorus, responding and sometimes revealing, and always expressing an alternate point of view. John Barth sees them associated with absent chapters. Of the six listed on the final page of the novel, he says, "[C]haracteristic is the dispatch with which he ends *Snow White*: a series of chapter-titles to which it would have been *de trop* to add the chapters themselves" (9).

To the question put to Snow White by the seven, "why do you remain with us? here? in this house?" she responds: "It must be laid, I suppose, to a failure of the imagination. I have not been able to imagine anything better." This answer pleases them, for they perceive it as a "powerful statement of our essential mutuality, which can never be sundered or torn, or broken apart, dissipated, diluted, corrupted or finally severed, not even by art in its manifold and dreadful guises" (59).

Which, of course, is dead wrong. "I have conflicting ideas," she says later. "But the main theme that runs through my brain is that what is, is insufficient" (135).

Snow White, 22, is a college graduate. A section describing her education, which she later refers to as her training in "the finest graces and arts" (102), reveals a conscious attempt to fashion herself in the image of a Renaissance woman: "She studied *Modern Woman, Her Privileges and Responsibilities*: the nature and nurture of women and what they stand for, in evolution and in history, including householding, upbringing, peacekeeping, healing and devotion, and how these contribute to the rehumanizing of today's world." And in typical Barthelme anticlimactic juxtaposition: "Then she studied *Classical Guitar I*, utilizing the models and techniques of Sor, Tarrega, Segovia, etc." This is followed by: "Then she studied *English Romantic Poets II*: Shelley, Byron, Keats" (25).

On the facing, preceding page, again giving the appearance of a chapter title with 14-point boldface capitals but in actuality yet another choral response, is the statement:

THE SECOND GENERATION OF ENG-
LISH ROMANTICS INHERITED THE

PROBLEMS OF THE FIRST, BUT COM-
PLICATED BY THE EVILS OF INDUSTRI-
ALISM AND POLITICAL REPRESSION.
ULTIMATELY THEY FOUND AN AN-
SWER NOT IN SOCIETY BUT IN VARI-
OUS FORMS OF INDEPENDENCE FROM
SOCIETY:

HEROISM

ART

SPIRITUAL TRANSCENDENCE (24).

Continuing on page 25: "Then she studied *Theoretical Foundations of Psychology*: mind, consciousness, unconscious mind, personality, the self, interpersonal relations, psychosexual norms, social games, groups, adjustment, conflict, authority, individuation, integration and mental health. Then she studied *Oil Painting I. . . ,*" followed by a list of the 12 paints she was told to bring to the first class. It goes on: "*Personal Resources I and II*: self-evaluation, developing the courage to respond to the environment, opening and using the mind, individual experience, training, the use of time, mature redefinition of goals, action projects," and, finally, "*Realism and Idealism in the Contemporary Italian Novel*" with a list of 17 Italian writers, and ending at a stroke with the fragment "Then she studied—"(25-26).

The eclecticism of all this reflects her superficiality. The original *Schneewittchen* or her Disney counterpart would never give a thought to being a Renaissance woman. This is a setup for failure, not only of imagination, as she says, but a failure of quest.

These odd and often funny juxtapositions of Barthelme's have a disjunctive function, quite the opposite of Hawthorne's embroidery of paranormal events onto history. Mentioned on page 41 are the following: a horror film, a sexual advance, a dry martini garnished with a pickled onion, a trout garnished with almonds, God, a Polish film, Snow White's reputation, and the name of an esoteric religious philosopher read by Snow White when she sulks in her room. Rather than flowing with the narrative, each of these stands apart, and, with the appearance of a name like Teilhard de Chardin, impedes it. The jackdaw again, a glittering accretion.

Snow White's seven housemates manufacture and distribute Chinese-style baby food with labels like *Baby Dow Shew,* bean curd stuffed with ground pike; *Baby Gai Goon,* chicken, bean sprouts and cabbage; and *Baby Pie Guat,* pork and oysters in soy sauce (18). Despite occasional ups and downs—"The grade of pork ears we are using in the Baby Ding Sam Dew is not capable of meeting U.S. Govt. standards, or indeed, any standards" (119)—the business has been lucrative: "It is amazing how many mothers will spring for an attractively packed jar of Baby Dim Sum, a tasty-looking potlet of Baby Jing Shar Shew Bow. Heigh-ho" (18). The recipes came from their father, who had always told them, "Try to be a man about whom nothing is known." Such a man was their father: "Nothing is known about him still. He gave us the recipes. He was not very interesting" (19).

The seven wonder how life would be if they got into another line of work: "God knows what. We do what we do without thinking. One tends the vats and washes the buildings and carries the money to the vault and never stops for a moment to consider that the whole process may be despicable." Before Snow White entered their lives, "There was equanimity for all. We washed the buildings, tended the vats, wended our way to the county cathouse once a week (heigh-ho). Like everybody else. We were simple bourgeois. We knew what to do." But everything has changed since the day the came upon her wandering in the forest, hungry and distraught, and gave her food. "Now we do not know what to do. Snow White has added a dimension of confusion and misery to our lives. Whereas once we were simple bourgeois who knew what to do, now we are complex bourgeois who are at a loss. We do not like this complexity" (87–88).

It is on a Monday that Snow White "let[s] down her hair black as ebony from the window." She says, "This motif, the long hair streaming from the high window, is a very ancient one I believe, found in many cultures, in various forms.

Now I recapitulate it, for the astonishment of the vulgar and the refreshment of my venereal life" (80).

The hair generates public reaction. Two old men remark, "'You need a Paul or Paul-figure for that sort of activity. Probably Paul is even now standing in the wings, girding his pants for his entrance'" (89).

Actually, Paul's in his bath, trying to get over a case of nerves caused by seeing the hair black as ebony on his way back from the Unemployment Office (94).

Snow White, meanwhile, becomes agitated by the 200 people watching her. She wishes she were on the beach at St. Tropez, "surrounded by brown boys without a penny. Here everyone has a penny. Here everyone worships the almighty penny." She laments: "O Jerusalem, Jerusalem! Thy daughters are burning with torpor and a sense of immense wasted potential, like one of those pipes you see in oil fields, burning off the natural gas that it isn't economically rational to ship somewhere!" (102).

Although this passage could be one of the targets of Barthelme's self-accusation, one joke too many (O'Hara 205), it does make the point that real men are in short supply for the daughters. In The Song of Songs (Song of Solomon in KJV) the chorus is called the Daughters of Jerusalem, and Barthelme, discussing in his *Paris Review* interview the attempt to reach the truth in writing, says that "our Song of Songs is the Uncertainty Principle" (O'Hara 200). This is not *blague*.

Another day comes and Snow White washes her hair with Golden Prell and again resorts to the routine of Rapunzel. Pondering "male domination of the physical world," she has gotten herself worked up. "Oh if I could just get my hands on the man who dubbed those electrical connections male and female! He thought he was so worldly. And if I could just get my hands on the man who called that piece of pipe a nipple! He thought he was so urbane." It was men who made a hash of the buffalo problem, who allowed the railroads to grab all the best land, and who let "alienation seep in everywhere and cover everything like a big gray electric blanket that doesn't work, after you have pushed the off-on switch to the 'on' position!" No one should accuse her of not being serious, she says. "Women may not be serious, but at least they're not a damned fool!" (131)

What she's doing is useless, she decides, and pulls in her hair. "No one has come to climb up. That says it all. This time is the wrong time for me. I am in the wrong time" (131). The usual crowd has gathered below her window. "There is something wrong with all those people standing there, gaping and gawking. And with all those who did not come and at least *try* to climb up. To fill the role. And with the very world itself, for not being able to supply a prince. For not being able to at least be civilized enough to supply the correct ending to the story" (132).

The final section of the book begins with another soliloquy by Snow White. Here, she vows chastity: "From now on I deny myself to them. These delights. I maintain an esthetic distance. No more do I trip girlishly to their bed in the night, or after lunch, or in the misty mid-morning."

Then she backpedals: "Not that I ever did. It was always my whim which governed those gregarious encounters summed up so well by Livy in the phrase, *vae victis* [woe to the conquered]. I congratulate myself on that score at least." No more, she says, "will I chop their onions, boil their fettucini, or marinate their flank steak. No more will I trudge about the house pursuing stain. No more will I fold their lingerie in neat bundles and stuff it away in the highboy." And what will this course of action win her? She's not sure (135), but clearly this is yet another move toward achieving the ideal.

THE DAYS OF DWARVES

Paul, though princely (or prince-figurely), cannot fill the heroic role. His destiny is to stop fleeing his destiny. On his way to a monastery in a remote part of Western Nevada where he intends to give himself up to a greater monarchy and draw robes from the supply room (116), he says, "If I had been born well prior to 1900, I could have ridden with Pershing against Pancho Villa. Alternatively, I could have ridden with Villa against the landowners and corrupt government officials of the time. In either case, I would have had a horse" (78).

Paul, like Snow White, always goes for form instead of content.

Snow White echoes this as she stands before a mirror, admiring her shape: "No wonder we who are twenty-two don't trust anybody over twelve. That is where you find people who know the score, under twelve. I think I will go out and speak to some eleven-year-olds, now, to refresh myself" (145).

Paul, she's determined, does not qualify as a prince. "Paul is frog. He is frog through and through." She has kept trying to believe that "he would, at some point, cast off his mottled wettish green-and-brown integument to reappear washed in the hundred glistering hues of princeliness. But he is *pure frog*. So. I am disappointed. Either I have overestimated Paul, or I have overestimated history" (169).

Or both.

This leaves Hogo de Bergerac, characterized by Barthelme as "a bad guy"(Brans 123).

Jane, with whom Hogo lives, calls him loathsome (32). "Hogo is not very simpatico—not much! He changed his name to Hogo from Roy and he wears an Iron Cross t-shirt. . . . His mother loved him when he was Roy, but now that he is Hogo she won't even speak to him, if she can help it" (32–33). Jane's mother warns, "Hogo is not the right type of young man for you to play with. He is thirty-five now and that is too old for innocent play. I am afraid he knows some kind of play that is not innocent, and then the fat will be in the fire" (57).

Jane disregards this advice because, she says, "Were it not for the fact that I am the sleepie of Hogo de Bergerac, I would be *total malice*. But I am redeemed by this hopeless love, which places me along the human continuum, still. Even Hogo is, I think, chiefly enamored of my malice" (40).   It's not long after this that she discovers large black stains on her new white-duck love seat with pillows of white-on-white Indian crewel. "That's all you know Hogo isn't it. How to take a thing that was white, and stain it until it is black. That's a pretty strong metaphor Hogo of what you would like to do with me, too. I understand" (113). The punctuation of this passage gives it the quality of an echo, suggesting that Jane's complaint lives on in Hogo's consciousness, long after it was uttered and with others of its kind.

Another metaphor is Hogo's own house and its chairs fashioned from Pontiac convertible seats—he drives a cobra-green Pontiac convertible— chain-link-fence walls, apes (their form never specified), and the ceiling covered with General Motors advertising materials (128). There is the ring of Robert Venturi humor here.

Hogo, the novel's antagonist, tells the seven early on: "Well chaps first I'd like to say a few vile things more or less at random, not only because it is expected of me but also because I enjoy it." He informs them that their housemate, Snow White, "is probably not worth worrying about" because her kind "grow like clams in all quarters of the world" and are "as multitudinous as cherrystones and littlenecks burrowing into the mud in all the bays of the world. The point is that the loss of any particular one is not to be taken seriously" (73–74).

"Male resentment," Barthelme says, "is a theme that's there" (Brans 123), but nevertheless, "Hogo's a thoroughly vile creature, or critter, and can be counted on to take the vilest possible view of things." Asked if Hogo is intended to corrupt the seven, Barthelme responds, "He's taken into partnership; that they're corrupted is not clear. He's efficient, a comment on efficiency" (O'Hara 205).

Hogo continues on his inspirational tack : "Ruin of the physical envelope is our great theme here, and if we keep changing girls every four or five years, it is because of this ruin, which I will never agree to" (Barthelme 74).

Hogo keeps an eye out, "to see what is passing, what has been cast up on the beach of our existence. Because something is always being cast up on that beach, as new classes of girls mature, and you can always get a new one, if you are willing to overlook certain weaknesses in the departments of thought and feeling." Any male wanting this, he points out, can always read a book, see a film or have an interior monologue. The spread of literacy has produced "girls who have thought and feeling too, in some measure, and some of them will probably belong to the Royal Philological Society or something, or in any case have their own 'thing,' which must be respected, and catered to, and nattered about, just as if you gave a shit about all this *blague.* " His main point, he says, "is that you should bear in mind multiplicity, and forget about uniqueness. The earth is broad, and flat, and deep, and high. And remember what Freud said" (75).

The section ends, leaving readers wondering just what that was, perhaps "Sometimes a cigar is just a cigar." But on the following page, set in boldface caps, is what Hogo is thinking of, presumably: "The value the mind sets on erotic needs instantly sinks as soon as satisfaction becomes readily available. Some obstacle is necessary to swell the tide of the libido to its height, and at all periods of history, whenever natural barriers have not sufficed, men have erected conventional ones" (76).

Hogo tells the seven to keep *multiplicity* in mind. This word alone throws light on his function in the novel and Barthelme's true purpose for him. It's obvious that Hogo isn't nearly as contemptible as he's made out to be. His attacks on females are ritualistic, and some of his other denunciations are deliberately specious. His illusory coarseness and outrageousness countervail the illusory highmindedness of Snow White and Paul, both of whom elevate fame above heroism.

"Which prince will come?" Snow White asks herself, and lists 31 possibilities ranging from Prince Hal to Prince Matchabelli. "Well it is terrific to be anticipating a prince," she says, "packed with grace" (77). And Paul sits in his eat-in kitchen, telling himself, "I am princely." And when he is feeling down, "I am able to pump myself up again by thinking about my blood. It is blue, the bluest this fading world has known probably" (27).

Sufficiently blue for Snow White, but what good is it if he cannot carry out the role? Both Snow White's position and that of Paul are devoid of passion—just more form over content, appearance above reality—while Hogo's position, which relies on the imagination, promises a better world than the one they're in. Hogo thus succeeds in counteracting Snow White and Paul.

But Hogo, who prefers "the viola da gamba-shaped Snow White" to Jane and her "cello shape" (152), is destined for rejection. "I must admit that your tall brutality has made its impression on me," Snow White tells him. "I am not unaffected by your Prussian presence, or by the chromed chains you wear looped around your motorcycle doublet, or by your tasteful scars on the left and right cheeks. But this 'love' must not be, because of your blood. You don't have the blood for this 'love,' Hogo. Your blood is not fine enough." She is not just anyone, she says; there is an expectation. "I am me. I must hold myself in reserve for a prince or prince-figure. . ." (170).

Blood is a strong argument, Hogo admits. "Yet in my blood there is a fever. I offer you this fever. It is as if my blood were full of St. Elmo's fire, so hot and electrical does it feel, inside me. If this fever, this rude but grand passion, in any measure ennobles me in your eyes, or in any other part of you, then perhaps all is not yet lost. . . ." But all is lost, she says. "It is simply a fever, in my view. Two aspirins and a glass of water" (170).

Hogo is, in a word, *vulgar*, but this is a word with more connections to *shared* and *vernacular* than *debased* (OED). His appearance represents imagination and passion, and this is the treasure he offers Snow White. The argument brings to mind, once again, Robert Venturi, calling for an architecture of eclecticism, ambiguity, and humor. Threaded through the narrative of *Snow White,* Hogo sometimes functions as a mouthpiece for Venturi.

In Venturi's "gentle manifesto" he says that he favors the hybrid over the pure, the compromising rather than the clean, distortion over the straightforward, the ambiguous rather than the articulated. He prefers the perverse, the impersonal, the boring and the interesting. Something conventional is preferable to something designed, the accommodating to the excluding, the redundant to the simple. He wants the vestigial as well as the innovating, the inconsistent and equivocal rather than the direct and clear. "I am," he declared, "for messy vitality over obvious unity. I include the non sequitur and proclaim the duality" (Venturi 16). More on Venturi in the next section.

This is what the double-minded Barthelme does in *Snow White*. He declares the duality with his version of Snow White attempting to morph herself onto the original, the ghostly images of Disney and the Brothers Grimm. This explains why Barthelme is careful to preserve the original, to deal with her as the specter, and form what John Barth calls "the alloy of irrealism and its opposite." It is achieved through whatever it is that Donald Barthelme contributes to narrative voice *in his time*. In this respect he is close to Hemingway.

Is Paul's line "What is the next thing demanded of me by history?" (55) something Barthelme wrestled with as a writer and felt an unrelenting urge to resist?

And there is Snow White's line: "This time is the wrong time for me. I am in the wrong time" (131). Is this true of Donald Barthelme himself? Was he, as it sometimes appears, a neoclassicist lost in time?

THE PLAYWRIGHT

In 1974, he drafted an adaptation of *Snow White* for the stage. His first attempt used lines from the published novel, but during the next two years he made cuts and added new material. In 1976 a third draft was done, this time with the assistance of American Place Theatre director Wynn Handman. A rehearsed reading was performed June 10, 1976 on Handman's stage in New York—its purpose, according to program notes, to give Barthelme "an opportunity to participate in rehearsals, see his play with an audience and hopefully use this experience to further the development of the play and of himself as a playwright"—this, according to Herzinger, a family friend.

Eleven days later Barthelme wrote a note of thanks to Handman: "The experience was invaluable to me. Not only did I learn what a poor play I had written, but also I got what I consider invaluable assistance in figuring out how it might be improved." Handman tried to persuade him to continue work on the play, but nothing more was ever done (Herzinger 351). Seven years later, his dialogue story "Great Days" was produced at the American Place Theatre. It opened on June 8, 1983 and closed June 26.

Not his cup of tea? Nothing ventured, nothing gained? It seems a great deal must have been lost. And Barthelme was not dabbling. He knew the stage would be ideal for some of his work—the dialogues and monologues—and he took very seriously what two of his fellow Postmodernists, the Austrians Peter Handke and Thomas Bernhard had been doing. In "Not-Knowing" he lists them among "alleged postmodernists"—himself, John Barth, William Gass, John Hawkes, Robert Coover, William Gaddis, and Thomas Pynchon, and Italy's Italo Calvino—all those trying to carry on the quest of Mallarmé to renew the language (116).

Though Bernhard and Handke differ in method and approach, both see language as a maximum-security "culture prison." Bernhard's most popular plays at the time of Barthelme's death were *The President* and *Eve of Retirement* (the latter premiered in 1981 at the Tyrone Gutherie Theatre in Minneapolis). In his dialogue Bernhard dispenses with punctuation because, he says, any mark creates a caesura. His translator Gitta Honegger calls this dialogue "a language that represents the death of its culture. It is a language after death, a language of relics (i.e., quotes) reconstituting a culture, society as artifice." In *Eve of Retirement* the dialogue shows how falsehoods of the past become so distorted in the process of being handed down that they can be made even to justify atrocities. This is evident as one character quotes her deceased father over and over while she and her brother, a former concentration camp commander, go about their yearly ritual of preparing to celebrate the birthday of Heinrich Himmler. In Bernhard's play *The President* another character continually quotes her friend, the chaplain, in weighty matters. Her husband explains:

> [S]he parrots whatever he says
> she doesn't understand what he says
> but she parrots it
> if the chaplain says dogs are innocent creatures
> she parrots it.

The chaplain's platitudes and truisms, we're told, come from "great French classics" that the cleric doesn't get quite right, but this doesn't really matter because Bernhard is arguing that the words have become lifeless anyway. Still, silence is not an option, neither for Bernhard nor for Handke (Bernhard-10–11).

Peter Handke's four actors—or *speakers*, as he refers to them—in *Offending the Audience* never appear to be at a loss for words.

> You will hear what you usually see.
> You will hear what you usually don't see.
> You will see no spectacle.
> Your curiosity will not be satisfied.
> You will see no play.
> There will be no playing here tonight.
> You will see a spectacle without pictures. (Handke 7)

From a bare stage, the actors hurl a total of 164 insults at their audience, one purpose being to remind them that they really are the audience (Hern 35–36). This, of course, is not acting in the conventional theatrical sense because there are no asides, illusions, destinies, dreams, factual reports, or slices of life, no story, actions, or world as stage. Not role-playing but mimesis: the actors are imitating the world and thus representing it. They tell the audience: "You are not playing along. You are being played with here. That is a wordplay . . . . You are the subject matter. You are the center of interest. No actions are performed here, you are being acted upon. That is no wordplay" (Handke 11–12).

They hammer away at the audience, calling them "an event . . . *the* event . . . the focal point . . . in the crossfire ... being inflamed . . . . You inflame us. Our words catch fire on you. From you a spark leaps across to us" (12).

As to time, "Only a now and a now and a now exist here. . . . Time plays no role here . . . . Time is for real here, it expires from one word to the next" (15).

Finally, it's down to business:

> While we are offending you, you won't just hear us, you will listen to us. The distance between us will no longer be infinite. . . . But we won't offend *you*, we will merely use offensive words which you yourselves use. We will contradict ourselves with our offenses. We will mean no one in particular. We will only create an acoustic pattern. . . . Since you are probably thoroughly offended already, we will waste no more time before thoroughly offending you, you chuckleheads (29)

Handke makes liberal use of the conventional theatrical devices of surprise, foiled expectations, and direct address—all involving role-playing, despite the many denials by the speakers. Hern parallels Handke's actors with those of Pirandello's *Six Characters in Search of an Author*[13]—both works have actors playing actors (29).

Handke's theatrical event is all about language, and by the closing minutes of the play, the language is anything but lifeless: "You had one of your better days tonight. You played ensemble. You were imitations of life, you drips, you diddlers, you atheists, you double-dealers, you switch-hitters, you dirty Jews" (30).

An argument put forth by Schlueter is that *Offending the Audience* is a complaint over the state of today's theater, that similar protest is found in all of

---

[13]*Sei personaggi in cerca d'autore*, 1921. Comedy in which the creations of art and the reality of life are intermingled. The rehearsal of a theater company is disrupted by a family, claiming to be characters from an unfinished dramatic work. They ask permission to reënact a crucial moment, so that the director might fashion a finished play.

Handke's plays and that, by design, he destroys in order to reconstruct (14–15). In the closing of the play, it's made clear that the audience has been on the stage all along:

> You were born actors. Play-acting was in your blood, you butchers, you buggers, you bullshitters, you bullies, you rabbits, you fuck-offs, you farts . . . . You crowned heads. You pushers. You architects of the future. You builders of a better world. You mafiosos. You wiseacres. You smarty-pants. You who embrace life. You who detest life. You who have no feeling about life. You ladies and gents you, you celebrities of public and culture life you, you who are present you, you brothers and sisters you, you comrades you, you worthy listeners you, you fellow humans you. (Handke 31–32).

Handke's play *Self-Accusation* was first performed in May 1968 on BBC Radio 3 and dedicated to John Lennon. It bears resemblance to *Offending the Audience* in its contrapuntal construction—that is, by introducing an idea early on and bringing it back later in a slightly different and more harmonious form—and in its performance on a bare stage with actors playing actors. Here, two speakers appear, a man and a woman, making statements in 41 paragraphs expressing guilt over events in their lives. Hern notes that the opening lines have an unmistakable "mock-biblical ring" that is consistent with the assortment of confessions that follow. But these "crimes against society" are harmless and have more to do with the personality of the speaker than anything else (48). Handke's purpose here is to undermine the value of the statements as confessions and make them "instead a proud assertion of individuality, and the final crescendo of irresponsible behavior in emergency conditions becomes an almost existential act of defiance in a chaotic world" (Hern 49).

Schlueter agrees. She says that the speakers' greatest sins are "self-expression, which has invariably conflicted with society's rules." The long list of wrongdoings "reminds the audience that this is the confession of a multitude of people, including the audience itself, individual members of which have undoubtedly committed some of these same sins" (Schlueter 33).

One speaker's list goes like this:

> I failed to observe the rules of the language. I committed
> linguistic blunders. I used words thoughtlessly. I blindly
> attributed qualities to the objects in the world. I blindly
> attributed to the words for the objects words for the qualities of
> the objects. I regarded the world blindly with the words for the
> qualities of the objects. I called objects dead. I called
> complexity lively. I called melancholy black. I called madness
> bright. I called passion hot. I called anger red. (Handke 44)

And, near the end of the play:

> I did not become what I ought to have become. I did not keep
> the promise that I could have kept. (49)

Considering any one of these four works as a whole, the case can be made
that the playwrights have succeeded in unbinding language and, perhaps, in
setting at least some of it free. Deconstructed, however, the pieces could seem to
be about themselves rather than the world, could appear to be guilty as charged, in
accordance with charges leveled against Postmodernist writing in general.
Barthelme lists a few of these in "Not-Knowing":

> The criticisms run roughly as follows: that this kind of writing has
> turned its back on the world, is in some sense not about the world
> but about its own processes, that it is masturbatory, certainly
> chilly, that it excludes readers by design, speaks only to the already
> tenured, or that it does not speak at all, but instead, like Frost's
> secret, sits in the center of a ring and Knows. (116)

Barthelme says of deconstruction that art in general relies on "a complex
series of interdependencies" and that any art can "illuminate just how strange the
combinatorial process can be." If the elements are isolated from the whole, he
contends, "in the interest of a finer understanding of same, the work will
collapse." He says that he does not find critical studies to be without value, but
"the mystery worthy of study, for me, is not the signification of parts but how
they come together" (119).

Which is to say, a Boeing 747 is not light in weight because its parts are. He says in the Brans interview that "a good piece will take on added presences that were perhaps not specifically built into it [and that] because of the new criticism, that intensely close reading, I think people did tend to read into pieces very often things that were not—and should not be—attributable to them" (136). In "Not-Knowing" he continues: "[I]n the competing methodologies of contemporary criticism, many of them quite rich in implications, a sort of tyranny of great expectations obtains, a rage for final explanations, a refusal to allow a work the mystery that is essential to it." The magic of something, he explains, "is that it at once invites and resists interpretation. Its artistic worth is measurable by the degree to which it remains, after interpretation, vital—meaning that no interpretation or cardiopulmonary push-pull can exhaust or empty it" (120).

In *The President, Eve of Retirement, Offending the Audience* and *Self-Accusation*, language is set at liberty, in large part, by the mystery posed by the speakers—their inconsistencies and contradictions, their riddles, paradoxes and questions, and the vicious circle they follow. The influence of *Self-Accusation* on Barthelme's *The Dead Father* is undeniable.

The Dead Father is one of John Gardner's targets in his 1978 attack on Postmodernist writers.

WORKS CITED IN THE CHAPTER

Arnason, H. H. *History of Modern Art.* New York: Harry N. Abrams, 1986.

Barth, John. "Thinking Man's Minimalist: Honoring Barthelme." *The New York Times Book Review*, 3 September 1989: 9.

Barthelme, Donald. "Not-Knowing." *Major Writers of Short Fiction: Stories and Commentaries.* Ann Charters, ed. Boston: Bedford Books of St. Martin's Press. 113–24.

———. *Snow White.* New York: Atheneum, 1972.

Bernhard, Thomas. *The President & Eve of Retirement.* Tr. Gitta Honegger. New York: Performing Arts Journal Publications, 1982.

Brans, Jo. "Embracing the World: An Interview with Donald Barthelme." *Southwest Review* 67, Spring 1982: 121–37.

Handke, Peter. *Kaspar and Other Plays.* Tr. Michael Roloff. New York: Farrar, Straus and Giroux, 1969.

Hern, Nicholas. *Peter Handke.* New York: Frederick Ungar Publishing Co., 1972.

Herzinger, Kim, ed. *The Teachings of Don B: Satires, Parodies, Fables, Illustrated Stories, and Plays of Donald Barthelme.* New York: Turtle Bay Books, 1992.

McCaffery, Larry. "An Interview with Donald Barthelme." *Anything Can Happen: Interviews with Contemporary American Novelists.* Ed. Thomas LeClair and McCaffery. Urbana: U of Illinois P, 1983. 32–44.

94

O'Hara, J. D. "Donald Barthelme: The Art of Fiction LXVI." *The Paris Review*, 1981: 180–210.

Schlueter, June. *The Plays and Novels of Peter Handke.* Pittsburgh: U of Pittsburgh P, 1981.

Venturi, Robert. *Complexity and Contradiction in Architecture*, 2nd ed. New York: Museum of Modern Art, 1977.

5 PUTTING POSTMODERNISM IN ITS PLACE

John Champlin Gardner's 1978 book *On Moral Fiction*, Barthelme complains in the 1982 Brans interview, "was clearly an attempt at a Saint Valentine's Day Massacre"[14] (129). He says little more about it, but considering the shift in his work during the 1980s—for example, in his 1986 novel *Paradise* the main character, a 53-year-old architect, is in spite of himself an optimist—a look at Gardner is appropriate. Some of what he says raises fundamental questions about literary Postmodernism itself.

Gardner died at 49 in a 1982 motorcycle accident. He is credited with 16 books, among them 11 novels, including *Grendel, Jason and Medeia, Nickel Mountain,* and *Mickelsson's Ghosts.* Everything he ever wrote reflects in some way his medievalist background. He taught most of his life, and his affiliations are listed as Oberlin, San Francisco State, Northwestern, Southern Illinois, Bennington, and the State University of New York-Binghamton. Among his scholarly works are two books on Chaucer. *On Becoming a Novelist* follows *On Moral Fiction,* and his final work, published posthumously, *The Art of Fiction,* softens or retreats from some of the charges made in *On Moral Fiction.*

Regarding the charges in *On Moral Fiction,* first impressions change on subsequent readings, and *how* he says these things becomes secondary to *what* he says. And whether it had results. Whether his attempt at a Saint Valentine's Day Massacre, cheap shot that it was, marked a turning point for the Postmodernist writers and for Donald Barthelme.

---

[14] The orchestrated elimination of the leaders of Bugs Moran's gang in 1929 left Al Capone leader of the Chicago underworld.

John Barth, looking back in his 1995 *Further Fridays: Essays, Lectures, and Other Nonfiction 1984-94*, refers to Gardner as "the novelist and polemicist" who

> laid into his fellow fiction writers at kneecap level with the AK-47 of "moral fiction": Nearly all of us, he charged, were delinquent in the fictive area of moral representation, which Gardner held to be the historical glory, indeed virtually the function, of fiction in general and the novel in particular. If one took him at his word, when the assault-rifle smoke cleared virtually no literary contemporary remained upright except the gunman himself.
> Those of us who cordially knew Gardner (and we were his principal targets) mainly sighed: There goes Bad John again, popping off his peers. (Barth 137)

BRINGING ORDER TO THE GUNFIGHT

It should be noted that all this heavy weapons imagery originates with Gardner himself. The book *On Moral Fiction* began life as an essay that appeared in the University of Chicago's *Critical Inquiry*, vol. 3, no. 4 (1977), under the title, "Death by Art: 'Some Men Kill You with a Six-gun, Some Men with a Pen.'" About halfway through *On Moral Fiction*, Gardner makes this tongue-in-cheek statement: "The gunfighting of artists is already common, of course. The fiercest and most interesting book reviews in the *New York Times* are by writers. My object here is therefore not to start up such gunfighting, or even to encourage it, but to make it a little more orderly, a little more deadly" (149). As Frederick the Great said at Prague in 1757: "No firing till you see the whites of their eyes."

Of Kurt Vonnegut, whose writing he calls "slight," Gardner says, "[H]is novels have the feel of first-class comic books (trash culture elevated to art, if you will) and can easily be read by people who dislike long sentences. Possibly Vonnegut is not telling the whole story when he speaks of his theory of keeping things short" (87).

On Joseph Heller: "Nothing happens in *Something Happened*" (88).

Saul Bellow fares no better: "We find a subtler kind of failure in the most admired of the old-fashioned moderns, Saul Bellow, actually not a novelist at heart but an essayist disguised as a writer of fiction" (91).

Early in the book, Gardner attacks William H. Gass:

> The best critical intelligence, capable of making connections the artist himself may be blind to, is a noble thing in its place; but applied to the making of art, cool intellect is likely to produce superficial work, either art which is all sensation or art which is all thought. We see this wherever we find art too obviously constructed to fit a theory, as in the music of John Cage or in the recent fiction of William Gass. (9)

But many would jump to defend Gass, including Charles Newman, in his 1985 *The Post-Modern Aura: The Act of Fiction in an Age of Inflation*:

> William Gass is the only contemporary American writer who has given us a coherent philosophy of fiction, an aesthetics which he actually practices, and a criticism coextensive with his art. His approach is apparently Formalist—tough-minded, polemical, proceeding through the entire panoply of relativism to purge the sentimental impulse—so that in the end the performance can be reaffirmed in impassioned holistic assertion. . . . (62)

Newman quotes the Gass philosophy from his *Fiction and the Figures of Life*: "The purpose of a literary work is the capture of consciousness . . . a consciousness electrified by beauty—is that not the aim and emblem and the ending of all finely made love? (Gass 33).

Gardner on Postmodernists in general: "[T]hese people . . . may be not so much a group of post-modernists as a gang of absurdists and jubilant nihilists, and perhaps also a few morally concerned writers whose innovative methods got them trapped in the wrong room" (54–55). The term *Postmodernism* not only "isolates a few writers and praises them beyond their due, depressing the stock of others or willfully misreading them; it judges cynical or nihilistic writers as characteristic of the age, and therefore significant, and thus supports, even celebrates ideas no father would willingly teach his children" (55–56).

A few pages later, Gardner once again narrows his sights on a specific target:

> Fiction as pure language (texture over structure) is *in*. It is one common manifestation of what is being called "post-modernism." At bottom the mistake is a matter of morality, at least in the sense that it shows, on the writer's part, a lack of concern. To people who care about events and ideas and thus, necessarily, about the clear and efficient statement of both, linguistic opacity suggests indifference to the needs and wishes of the reader and to whatever ideas may be buried under all that brush. And since one reason we read fiction is our hope that we will be moved by it, finding characters we can enjoy and sympathize with, an academic striving for opacity suggests, if not misanthropy, a perversity or shallowness that no reader would tolerate except if he is one of those poor milktoast innocents who timidly accept violation of their feelings from a habit of supposing they must be missing something, or one of those arrogant donzels who chuckle at things obscure because their enjoyment proves to them that they are not like lesser mortals. Where language is of primary concern to the writer, communication is necessarily secondary. Gass is handy proof.
> (69)

Quoting at length from the philosophic-poetic essay *On Being Blue,* calling it "beautiful," Gardner adds that a little goes a long way because "Gass does not move from this to translucency" (70).

Opacity and *translucency* are key here.

> Gass is not alone, though he's the best of the lot, or at least the most stubbornly unreadable and thus most widely read by students and professors who admire opacity. Mobs of contemporary writers—writers very different in other respects—follow Gass in focusing their attention on language, gathering nouns and verbs the way a crow collects paper clips, sending off their characters and action to take a long nap. J. P. Dunleavy, Ron Sukenick, James Purdy, Stanley Elkin, John Barth, and a good many more of our writers concentrate, to a greater or lesser extent, on language for its own sake, more in love, on principle, with the sound of words—or with newfangledness—than with creating fictional worlds. One might say, in their defense, that what they create is "linguistic sculpture," or one might argue that some of this tightly wedged,

cockleburred fiction goes beautifully, like *Finnegans Wake*, when read aloud. (Even about *Wake* one may, of course, have reservations.) But the fact remains that the search for opacity has little to do with the age-old search for understanding and affirmation. Linguistic sculpture at best makes only the affirmation sandcastles make, that it is pleasant to make things or look at things made, better to be alive than dead. (Gardner 70–71)

This is not without its good points, but one wishes that Gardner had left it at that and not said, "The more time one spends piling up words, the less often one needs to move from point to point, argument to argument, or event to event; that is, the less need one has of structure"(71). What he seems to miss is that the argument of translucency versus opacity is not about word count but harmony.

After this attack, one might wonder if only Gardner is left standing:

The generous critic might hold up numerous other writers as important artists—John Barth, Thomas Pynchon, Joyce Carol Oates, Robert Coover, Donald Barthelme, James Purdy, William Gaddis, John Hawkes, Katherine Anne Porter, Guy Davenport, John Cheever, Bernard Malamud, J. D. Salinger, Eudora Welty, and John Updike, to name a few. How many of them will outlast the century? Perhaps Malamud, certainly a powerful artist at his best; conceivably Guy Davenport, if sheer precision and uncompromising artistry count, but his output is spare and his work goes underadvertized; possibly Eudora Welty, because of one superb novel, *Losing Battles*, a handful of stories, and her secure position as Southerner and woman in our college American literature courses; possibly Joyce Carol Oates, for a few excellent short stories; possibly Salinger. But I suspect that what I've typed above is a list of inflated reputations. Some on the list will die quickly, of pure meanness—Porter, Coover, and Gaddis—and some will die of intellectual blight, academic narrowness, or fakery—Pynchon, Updike (or most of his work), and Barth (94).

He takes Northrop Frye to task, saying, that he "is claiming, as the New Criticism regularly claimed, that what counts in literature is not what it says, what it affirms and promulgates, but only how well it works as a self-contained, organic whole busy doing whatever it does." While this position, "all but universal in the past few decades," has some truth, Gardner says, it "leaves out art's primary business: direct or indirect (ironic) affirmation" and "refuses to investigate why *The Iliad* is the greatest single poem in our tradition, or why Shakespeare at his worst is better than de Sade at his best. It shrugs off such questions because it thinks it knows the answer: beauty is truth is relative" (131–32).

Barth, from a 1990 vantage, looks back, but not in anger:

> Self-serving as his tirade was, however, it was by no means merely so. The man earnestly believed, I think, that the likes of Vladimir Nabokov, Donald Barthelme, William Gass, John Hawkes, Thomas Pynchon, and myself were perpetrating not immoral but amoral fiction—and that in this we were reprehensible.
>
> While not happy to be thus consigned to Hell, I for one was honored to have such splendid company in the Circle of Literary Irresponsibles. On the other hand, I felt that there was enough to be said for Gardner's argument that it deserved a keener arguer: one who would not only choose his targets more judiciously (I see much exemplary morality in the writers named above, and much clunky art in the more programmatically "moral" novelists) but would also distinguish more consistently between the moral *aspect* of most great literature, which I readily affirm, and the notion of a writer's moral *duty*, which I resist. . . (137).

To Barthelme, Gardner devotes almost three pages. Of the new writers, he says, whose work can be characterized as

> holding up a mirror to the age, the best is perhaps Donald Barthelme. He has a sharp eye for modern man's doubts and anxieties, free-floating guilt, politics, manners, turns of speech. In much of his fiction he aims at simple imitation in the form of comic-expressionistic cartoon. At times (as in "The Explanation"), he seems to aim at a certain kind of satire, but it's the satire of despair, not grounded on theory, implied in the work, of what ought to be, but constructed out of bemused weariness, irascibility, New York stylishness, and, sometimes, disgust. Both in drawings and in fictions, he imitates cleverly the modern world's sadness and confused sense of fear and loss, and in even the most fabulous or refracted of his fictions he keeps a careful eye on how the world really works. (79–80)

"The Explanation," first collected in Barthelme's 1970 *City Life,* has two male speakers, Q and A, with the former questioning and at times instructing the latter on an unidentified, mysterious machine—some variety of computer, since Q associates error messages with it—the front panel represented on the page by a black square. This, of course, is part of the joke. It's unfathomable, like nearly everything else Q and A discuss: the death of the novel, A's sweater, complete sexual satisfaction from a pill, the content of Maoism, and madness as an alternative to reason.

Q has an unspecified role in the building of the machine, but A is simply not interested in machines. "What are your interests?" Q asks him, and his reply is equally inscrutable: "I'm a director of the Schumann Festival" (*40 Stories* 41). A's interests lie in an attractive female he claims to have seen crossing the street and with whom he had brief eye contact. "I want to go back and do it again," he tells Q. There is a break and then:

> Q: Now that you've studied it for a bit, can you explain how it works?
> A: Of course. (Explanation)
> Q: Is she still removing her blouse?
> A: Yes, still.

That's it for the Explanation, whatever it is, presumably the encounter. Q questions A as to the woman's progress with the blouse. It never comes off, although she does remove everything else and walks along a log carrying her sunglasses in her hand. A tells Q that she is "quite beautiful" (41).

A can discuss this woman, as she exists in his mind, and not be proved wrong, as he certainly would be in discussing the purity of Maoism (41) or baseball (44). Even a picture of his daughter he holds up for Q to see is represented on the page by the same black square (44). But the female walking the log, for him, is immutable; it is what defines him, and this is The Explanation.

Satire, to be sure, but not the satire of despair, as Gardner charges. Nor is there "bemused weariness, irascibility, New York stylishness, and, sometimes, disgust" (Gardner 79). Boredom, yes, as seen in this self-referential exchange:

> Q: Are you bored with the question-and-answer form?
> A: I am bored with it but I realize that it permits many valuable omissions: what kind of day it is, what I'm wearing, what I'm thinking. That's a very considerable advantage, I would say.
> Q: I believe in it. (39)

Gardner goes on to say that Barthelme "has all the qualities of 'talent' which Tolstoy[15] listed in his early 'Introduction to the Works of Guy de Maupassant'"—these being, first, "a correct, that is, a moral relation of the author to his subject"; second, "clearness of expression, or beauty of form—the two are identical"; and finally, "sincerity, that is, a sincere feeling of love or hatred of what the artist depicts"—but in Barthelme, "all three qualities are enfeebled. He knows what is wrong, but he has no clear image of, or interest in, how things ought to be. . . . The world would be a duller place without him, as it would be without F. A. O. Schwartz. But no one would accuse him of creating what Tolstoy called 'religious art'" (80).

And here Gardner makes his most damning accusation:

> His world is not one of important values but only of values mislaid, emotions comically or sadly unrealized, a burden of mysteries no one has the energy to solve. It is a world he seems to have little wish to escape; or if one of his characters feels an urge to transcend the limitations of his world . . . we get only the resolve and promise, seldom the act. His writing has emotional control, clarity of style, and at least an impression of life's tragic waste; but even at his best, as in *The Dead Father*, Barthelme goes not for the profound but for the clever.
>
> The limitation evident in a writer like Barthelme—and many lyric poets—is not moral shallowness, as it may first seem, but a species of Romantic self-love. Though I have said that he holds up a mirror to his age, Barthelme' s effectiveness as a writer of fiction does not lie—as did the power of Tolstoy or Henry James—in seeing into other people's minds, even people the writer dislikes,

---

[15] Gardner's citation: Tolstoy, Leo. *What Is Art? and Essays on Art.* Tr. Aylmer Maude. London: Oxford U P, 1969. 21.

and recreating diverse lives on paper, giving each character his moment of dignity and thus helping us to understand intellectually and intuitively both others and ourselves. (80–81)

Barthelme, asked in 1980 about "psychological studies" in his writing, responds: "I'm not so interested. 'Going beneath the surface' has all sorts of positive-sounding associations, as if you were a Cousteau of the heart. I'm not sure there's not just as much to be seen if you remain a student of the surfaces" (McCaffrey 43).

In the 1981 O'Hara interview, to the question "Don't you write more about the mind than about the external world?" his answer is: "In a commonsense way, you write about the impingement of one upon the other—my subjectivity bumping into other subjectivities, or into the Prime Rate. You exist for me in my perception of you (and in some rough, Raggedy Ann way, for yourself, of course). That's what's curious when people say, of writers, this one's a realist, this one's a surrealist, this one's a super-realist, and so forth. In fact, everybody's a realist offering true accounts of the activity of the mind. There are only realists" (O'Hara 200–1).

Gardner finally gets around to labeling Barthelme:

> Barthelme reflects his doubting and anxious age because he is, himself, an extreme representative of it. In this as in everything, it is worth noticing, he is a typical minor Romantic. Whereas for Montaigne or Wordsworth meditation on the self aims toward knowledge of humanity in general, and whereas for Pascal the self is hateful, getting in the way of communion with God, the minor Romantic is an egoist. At best he claims that, miserable as he may be, he's a model for imitation: better to be disillusioned than deluded. At worst he claims, as Rousseau did in his *Confessions*, "I am not like any one of those I've seen; I dare say I am unlike any man that exists." The modern Narcissus dreams up no large goals for all humanity because he's chiefly interested in his own kinks, pathetic or otherwise; and ironically, what a careful study of freaks reveals is that they're all alike. As we recognize our own moments of despair in the unmitigated gloom of Beckett, we recognize in all sad and weary writers common elements of ourselves, mainly our weakness. (81)

For Gardner, moral art has to be social, "at least by implication. . . and on the other hand, there can be no moral social art . . . without honesty in the individual—the artist—as a premise for just and reasonable discussion" (82).

> Moral art in its highest form holds up models of virtue, whether they be heroic models like Homer's Achilles or models of quiet endurance, like the coal miners, the steelworkers, the Southern midwife, or the soldiers in the photographs of W. Eugene Smith. The artist so debilitated by guilt and self-doubt that he cannot be certain real virtues exist is an artist doomed to second-rate art, an artist of whom the best that can he said is that he's better, at least, than the consciously nihilistic artist or (worse, perhaps) the artist who believes in morality but has got it all wrong, so that he holds up for emulation what ought to be despised. (82)

Barthelme says, "I do believe that my every sentence trembles with morality—it's full of morality. But it's the morality of an attempt. It's not the morality of giving you precepts. To decide as Gardner would that my enterprise is immoral because it doesn't preach to you or elevate you in some dubious way—."

The interviewer interrupts him with a question, but he continues the statement later: "And you're not going to persuade me that making art is not a highly moral act in itself. It's certainly difficult enough to qualify as a moral act" (Brans 129).

To O'Hara, he insists that his work is moral because it "attempts to engage the problematic rather than to present a proposition to which all reasonable men must agree. The engagement might be very small . . . 'mess around' for 'covet,' which undresses adultery a bit. I think the paraphrasable content in art is rather slight—'tiny,' as de Kooning puts it" (199).

Great art, according to Gardner,

> celebrates life's potential, offering a vision unmistakably and unsentimentally rooted in love. "Love" is of course another of those embarrassing words, perhaps a word even more embarrassing than "morality," but it's a word no aesthetician ought carelessly to drop from his vocabulary. Misused as it may be by

pornographers and the makers of greeting-cards, it has, nonetheless, a firm, hard-headed sense that names the single quality without which true art cannot exist. It is a quality that shouts from the sculptures of Thomas Mallory, the music of Benjamin Britten and, among younger composers, Joseph Baber, and from good novels both slight and monumental—from John Irving or Toni Morrison to Italo Calvino or Thomas Mann. (83–84)

Echoing Joseph Campbell, Gardner says that myths are needed.

Real art creates myths a society can live instead of die by, and clearly our society is in need of such myths. What I claim is that such myths are not mere hopeful fairy tales but the products of careful and disciplined thought; that a properly built myth is worthy of belief, at least tentatively; that working at art is a moral act; that a work of art is a moral example. . . (126).

He ends with:

True art's divine madness is shot through with love: love of the good, a love proved not by some airy and abstract high-mindedness but by active celebration of whatever good or trace of good can be found by a quick and compassionate eye in this always corrupt and incorruptible but god-freighted world (204–205).

Barthelme, asked what he considered the proper response to the world, answers: "Embracing it" (Brans 132).

STEPPING OUT OF REALITY

In both *The Art of Fiction* and *On Moral Fiction*, Gardner mentions Barthelme's story "Paraguay," also in the *City Life* collection. In *On Moral Fiction* he brands it as empty, as form without content, insisting that

he simply steps out of reality to play with the literary conventions which once helped us learn about the real. His form is elegant, but it suggests no beauty beyond literary shape, as if workmanship were now enough, there being no real value for that workmanship to struggle toward (only death for it to struggle against). And his sincerity is, though authentic, remote: he cares not about people but about ideas or "constructs"—in effect, painterly images: the Phantom of the Opera, Snow White more or less realistically conceived (neurotic modern life played against myth). His diagnosis of the evils of the age can be amusing, and perhaps, for some readers, moving. (80)

In the story, "The Phantom of the Opera's Friend," the Phantom alternates between hubris and despair (bipolar disorder, by the look of it) and so wears down the author—the Phantom's "friend"—that for the sake of his own sanity he feels he must abandon the project, *The Phantom of the Opera,* and move on to another, *The Secret of the Yellow Room.* Barthelme has Gaston Leroux carefully place the *Phantom* manuscript on a shelf in the closet and pull out a clean sheet of foolscap, on top of which he writes *The Secret of the Yellow Room.* These two works, an assemblage of diverse elements, are linked by the Phantom as he reacts to being put on the shelf (*60 Stories* 138–43).

As to "Paraguay," Charles Newman's earlier observation is worth repeating here:

> The hallmark of a Barthelme story . . . whatever its quality, is that it is *essentially unparodyable.* Think of the consequences of that— anticipating every objection in its very rhythms, a work of art which will not yield to further mimicry. Within its own context it can only be imitated: neither totally assimilated nor challenged; the *ne plus ultra* of daemonic irony, the end of the road of interiority (79).

"Paraguay" begins like a travelogue, imitating the style of *National Geographic* travel stories, especially the more exotic treatments that appeared in the early part of the twentieth century:

> The upper part of the plain that we had crossed the day before was now white with snow, and it was evident that there was a storm raging behind us and that we had only just crossed the Burji La in time to escape it. We camped in a slight hollow at Sekbachan, eighteen miles from Malik Mar, the night as still as the previous one and the temperature the same; it seemed as if the Deosai Plains were not going to be so formidable as they had been

described; but the third day a storm of hail, sleet, and snow
alternately came at noon when we began to ascend the Sari Sangar
Pass, 14,200 feet, and continued with only a few minutes'
intermission till four o'clock. (*60 Stories* 127)

This travel guide-narrator is planting inconsistencies, most of which are not
immediately apparent. The snow on the upper plain—how does he know a *raging*
storm was responsible? He says it's "evident" but describes the night the storm
occurred as being "still." And the Burji La is some kind of boundary, an obstacle
requiring special effort to cross. It could be a deep gorge or a high ridge. Then
comes a weather phenomenon, an unprecedented storm of alternating hail, sleet,
and snow. And the top of a 14,200-foot pass that is "a fairly level valley
containing two lakes." But it cannot be level if the shores of those lakes are
"formed of boulders that seemed impossible to ride over" (127).

What Gardner failed to understand (or wanted us to believe he didn't) was
that out of all this seeming incoherence, patterns emerge and act as binding
forces, beckoning us on, luring us to follow the assemblage of elements—a trail
of debris, some would say—that gives this story the ability to fascinate.

Still in the first paragraph, the narrator and his men reach a cairn at the
summit, where, he explains, "it is customary to give payment to the coolies. I paid
each man his agreed-upon wage, and, alone, began the descent. Ahead was
Paraguay."

And the word *Paraguay* has a footnote: "Quoted from *A Summer Ride
Through Western Tibet,* by Jane E. Duncan, Collins, London, 1906. Slightly
altered." There is such a book listed in the Library of Congress catalog.

The string of incongruities here help make up the poetic language of the
piece. Gardner misses this point with his concern that Barthelme "play[s] with the
literary conventions which once helped us learn about the real," and that
paradoxes do not contribute to character. It's true that at the end, the reader knows
next to nothing about the travel guide-narrator, and not much more about the
woman Jean Mueller. But the growing consciousness in the story is that of the

reader, not of the characters, and it's the continual disorientation that serves as the complicating action—exactly what Barthelme intended.

"Paraguay" follows the pattern of other Barthelme stories, where the task is not problem-solving but question-posing. Barthelme has said that he sees his job as taking an answer and coming up with a riddle. His quest is for the question, he says—the right one "that will generate light and heat" (O'Hara 198). The elements of his "Paraguay" collage pose the question.

He has dissimilar material of almost equal length organized under 14 italicized headings: *Where Paraguay Is, Jean Mueller, Temperature, Herko Mueller, Error, Rationalization, Skin, The Wall, Silence, Terror, The Temple, Microminiaturization, Behind the Wall,* and *Departure.*

Under the heading *Where Paraguay Is*, the narrator begins with, "Thus I found myself in a strange country."

He explains what and where it's not:

"This Paraguay is not the Paraguay that exists on our maps. It is not to be found on the continent, South America; it is not a political subdivision of that continent, with a population of 2,161,000 and a capital city of Asunción. This Paraguay exists elsewhere" (128).

Elsewhere—the adverb that keeps showing up in Barthelme's writings. With tension building, it has percussive power, and he extends the momentum by having his narrator, "tired but also elated and alert," making his way toward "the first of the 'silver cities'"—referring to Le Corbusier[16] and his radiant city design—and observing that "Flights of white meat moved through the sky overhead in the direction of the dim piles of buildings" (128).

---

[16] Architectural pseudonym, taken from his family history, of the Swiss Charles-Édouard Jeanneret (Poole 122). His "Radiant City" project had vertical dwellings, each housing more than 1,500 people (133). He believed that collective living was ideal for humankind and assured in these multi-level dwellings, "seclusion, silence, and rapidity of 'inside-outside' contacts." Le Corbusier rejected the notion that human beings, by nature, are social and need the community of a neighborhood (134).

This is only the second paragraph of the story, but already Barthelme has succeeded in transmogrifying a James-Hilton-Shangri-La canvas to this surreal one that, as more and more diverse elements accumulate, develops into a flawed Utopia.

Up until now, place names have connected all this apparent discontinuity, but here a character is introduced to carry on with the job. The sentence about "Flights of white meat" functions as a transition to the section that follows, titled *Jean Mueller.*

The narrator encounters a person he describes as "a dark girl wrapped in a red shawl," the edges fringed, each strand tipped with "a bob of silver"—who "at once placed her hands on my hips, standing facing me; she smiled, and exerted a slight pull. I was claimed as her guest; her name was Jean Mueller" (Barthelme 128). Again, disjunctions, spliced with semicolons. Things are even more out of whack here, because unless the silver bobs on every strand of that shawl were the size of buckshot, poor Jean would be pulled to the ground.

And local hospitality manifests itself: by putting her hands on *his* hips, she *claimed* him. For what we shall soon discover.

They go to her house, "a large modern structure some distance from the center of the city." Jean Mueller shows him to his room, among its furnishings a "handsome piano in a cherrywood case." She tells him that after he rests he *might* join her downstairs and *might* then meet her husband. The tentativeness here has to do with the Paraguayan value system, which turns out to be wholly ambiguous. "We try to keep everything open," Jean tells him, and to "go forward avoiding the final explanation" (Barthelme 132). This can only mean *no* explanation and, therefore, no understanding.

As Jean Mueller is about to leave, she sits down at the piano, and, "almost mischievously, played a tiny sonata of Bibblemann's" (128). No matter Bibblemann's identity, how can a sonata, which is supposed to have three movements of different tempo, be tiny?

The canvas is getting cluttered, but, of course, this is collage. Recall what Barthelme said about it, that dissimilar components can be put down on the canvas with the hope of making a new reality. This is what he's doing—in an incredible parody of popular culture with its institutionalized art and architecture.

He takes a first swing at the Modernist school of architecture with his reference to "the dim piles of buildings," and slams the art establishment by describing the systematic production of art in Paraguay. Under the heading *Rationalization*, the narrator tells how it's done in Paraguay:

> The problems of art. New artists have been obtained. These do not object to, and indeed argue enthusiastically for, the rationalization process. Production is up. Quality-control devices have been installed at those points where the interests of artists and audience intersect. Shipping and distribution have been improved out of all recognition. (It is in this area, they say in Paraguay, that traditional practices were most blameworthy.) The rationalized art is dispatched from central art dumps to regional art dumps, and from there into the lifestreams of cities. Each citizen is given as much art as his system can tolerate. (130)

The following extract, full of jargon and high-tech gobbledygook from manufacturing and computer engineering, makes for stark narrative about mini-malization of art in Paraguay and the rules to implement it:

> Marketing considerations have not been allowed to dictate product mix; rather, each artist is encouraged to maintain, in his software, highly personal, even idiosyncratic, standards (the so-called "hand of the artist" concept). Rationalization produces simpler circuits and, therefore, a saving in hardware. Each artist's product is translated into a statement in symbolic logic. The statement is then "minimized" by various clever methods. The simpler statement is translated back into the design of a simpler circuit. (130)

The finishing process is no less methodical:

> Foamed by a number of techniques, the art is then run through heavy steel rollers. Flip-flop switches control its further development. Sheet art is generally dried in smoke and is dark

brown in color. Bulk art is air-dried, and changes color in particular historical epochs. (130)

The insinuation is unmistakable. Certain art galleries do engage in the systematic production and distribution of fine art, and Barthelme mimics their catalogs here, using "back-broke" sentences, one of those ungainly constructions with an eye on greatness (McCaffrey 34).

Everything in Paraguay appears rule-driven, even the air temperature at which sexual intercourse can occur—66 to 69 degrees—"and only within that scale"(Barthelme 129). "Sexual life is very free. There are rules but these are like the rules of chess, intended to complicate and enrich the game" (133).

Paraguay is not without problems. A "government error resulting in the death of a statistically insignificant portion of the population (less than one-fortieth of one per cent) has made people uneasy." Another problem, the narrator says, is that of shedding skin: "Thin discarded shells like disposable plastic gloves are found in the street" (130).

The episode under the heading *Skin* is not soon forgotten.

> Ignoring a letter from the translator Jean sat on a rubber pad doing exercises designed to loosen the skin. Scores of diamond-shaped lights abraded her arms and legs. The light placed a pattern of false information in those zones most susceptible to tearing. Whistling noises accompanied the lights. The process of removing the leg skin is private. Tenseness is eased by the application of a cream, heavy yellow drops like pancake batter. I held several umbrellas over her legs. A man across the street pretending not to watch us. Then the skin placed in the green official receptacles. (131)

This, then, is what Jean claimed him for, not sex.

In the section entitled *The Wall* a second footnote appears: "Quoted from *The Modular,* by Le Corbusier, MIT Press, Cambridge, 1954. Slightly altered" (131). A "vast blind wall" is described, "the danger of having a dreary expanse of blankness" relieved by placing a stone and the "Stele of the Measures" in front of it. "The wall would be divided, by means of softly worn paths, into doors. These, varying in size from the very large to the very small, would have different colors and thicknesses. Some would open, some would not, and this would change from week to week, or from hour to hour. . ." (131).

Under the heading *Behind the Wall,* in this allusion to Georg Büchner's *Woyzeck,* which Barthelme once praised in a *New Yorker* film review, the narrator reports:

> Behind the wall there is a field of red snow. I had expected that to enter it would be forbidden, but Jean said no, walk about in it as much as you like. I had expected that walking in it one would leave no footprints, or that there would be some other anomaly of that kind, but there were no anomalies; I left footprints and felt the cold of red snow underfoot. I said to Jean Mueller, "What is the point of this red snow?"

A question that could apply to Paraguay itself. And be answered thus:

> "The intention of the red snow, the reason it is isolated behind the wall, yet not forbidden, is its soft glow—as if it were lighted from beneath. You must have noticed it; you've been standing here for twenty minutes." "But what does it do?" "Like any other snow, it invites contemplation and walking about in."

And after one walks through it:

> The snow rearranged itself into a smooth, red surface without footprints. It had a red glow, as if lighted from beneath. It seemed to proclaim itself a mystery, but one there was no point in solving—an ongoing low-grade mystery. (134)

Much of the mystery of this story can be solved by looking at architectural history, the changing of the guard, the fall of Modernism and heralding of Postmodernism. An event some believe to mark the end of Modernism in architecture actually occurred after the publication of "Paraguay," but everyone, including Barthelme, knew it was coming. Arnason writes that the International Style had become ascendant in the flurry of construction following World War II, holding "virtually totalitarian power over architects and clients alike." The influential Modernist International style spread over Europe and the U.S. during the 1920s and 1930s. It can be identified by its symmetrical, plain geometric forms and open interiors, and the use of steel, reinforced concrete, and glass.

The coup de grâce was administered, it is said, on July 15, 1972, when the Pruitt-Igoe public-housing project in St. Louis was demolished by dynamite "after all other measures had failed to save this monument to rational, Utopian, Bauhaus planning from the social and economic horror it had become." The project had been built 20 years before, a "sleek modernist complex" that won for its designer, Minoru Yamasaki, the American Institute of Architects' award:

> Complete with "streets in the air," safe from automobile traffic, and access to "sky, space, and greenery," which Le Corbusier had deemed the "three essential joys of urbanism," Pruitt-Igoe offered all, including purist styling, that enlightened, idealistic specialists had assumed would inspire, by example, a sense of virtue in the inhabitants. By the end of the 1960s, however, the clinically smart, multi-million dollar fourteen-story slab blocks had become so vandalized, crime-ridden, squalid, and dysfunctional that only their demolition could solve the manifold problems. The best of modernist thought, owing to its aloof indifference to the small-scale, personal requirements of privacy, individuality, context, and sense of place, could do nothing to make Pruitt-Igoe Housing a workable home for the economically disadvantaged persons whose living conditions it was meant to improve.

In the view of the Architectural Postmodernists, Arnason says,

> the followers of Miës, Gropius, and Le Corbusier had created a movement far too narrowly ideological, collectivist, hard-edged, and impersonal—certain too self-referential in its insistence upon formalism dictated purely by function and technology—to give satisfaction in a society whose diversity could only become more pronounced with the arrival of the "Me Generation."

Form without content, the charges went, whereas the new movement,

> has a voracious appetite for an irrational, eclectic mix of history, vernacular expression, decoration and metaphor. Moreover, Post-Modernists seek to build in relation to everything, the site and its established environment, the client's specific needs, including

those of wit and adventure in living, historical precedent relevant to current circumstance, and communicable symbols for the whole enterprise. (Arnason 691)

Venturi, that same year, 1972, was calling for a study of contemporary "vernacular architecture" such as that found on the Las Vegas strip, urging that it is "as important to architects and urbanists today as were the studies of medieval Europe and ancient Rome and Greece to earlier generations." There is much to be learned from this landscape, he says, because it represents "a new type of urban form, radically different from that which we have known, one which we have been ill-equipped to deal with which, from ignorance, we define today as urban sprawl." In the opinion of Venturi, "the seemingly chaotic juxtaposition of honky-tonk elements expresses an intriguing kind of vitality and validity" (Arnason 691–93).

> Venturi's Postmodern structures, Guild House, 1960–63, among them, Trachtenberg calls the "clearest visual equivalent" to Barthelme's fiction (19). Guild House is a block of 91 apartments for elderly residents of an old section of Philadelphia. Venturi gave this edifice the utilitarian, dark-red-brick look of the typical urban renewal project, which blended well with this inner-city neighborhood's commercial character. But Guild House, Arnason says, "evinces some of the nobility of a princely residence or a Baroque church" and it "provided a beacon for younger architects seeking a new architecture of 'inclusion'—an architecture at home in the existing environment, combining features of the average, everyday building and historical styles . . . the ordinary with the sophisticated" (Arnason 693).

The mixture here is significant and gives strength to the argument that Postmodernism is not so much a break with Modernism as a disruption of it, using aesthetic practices intended to undermine ingrained attitudes and to question concepts and assumptions.

With this in mind, "Paraguay" is a good example of the Barthelme alloy of irrealism and its opposite. Gardner, in *The Art of Fiction*, refers to the story as "formalist irrealism" (136). Earlier in the book he contends that literary

Postmodernism "sets up only a vague antithesis to 'modernism,' meaning only, in effect, more like Italo Calvino than like Saul Bellow" (86). Barth says, [I]f the irrealist happens to be Italo Calvino, deal me in" (141).

Barth is not alone in this. Calvino is revered—without regard to Postmodernism—especially among the young.

THE IRREALIST'S IRREALIST

Barthelme consistently praised Calvino, who like the other Postmodernists named in "Not-Knowing," carried on the battle of Mallarmé to renew a dull and oftentimes tarnished language (116). Hume believes Calvino to be resolute in this, that for him language is a barricade between one's consciousness and the exterior, whether it's a relationship or the cosmos (145). In two of his novels, *Mr. Palomar,* 1983, and *Invisible Cities,* 1972, he has his protagonists making the trip from the interior of consciousness, but in the way he prowls the imagination looking for eternity, he's more Sterne-like than Modernist. The irony of these novels, their self-consciousness, indeterminacy and immanence place them within the perimeter of the Postmodernist camp.

Early in his novel *Mr. Palomar*, Calvino attempts to connect the human mind to the universe when he has his protagonist, while taking an evening swim, make the following revelation: "All this is happening not on the sea, not in the sun . . . but inside my head, in the circuits between eyes and brain. I am swimming in my mind; this sword of light exists only there; and this is precisely what attracts me. This is my element, the only one I can know in some way" (15).

Here is one connection to "Not-Knowing," that the journey to discovery is one of the greatest stories in literature. In the essay Barthelme explains that the state of "not-knowing is crucial to art, is what permits art to be made. Without the scanning process engendered by not-knowing, without the possibility of having the mind move in unanticipated directions, there would be no invention" (113). This is Calvino.

The Cuban-born Calvino in two of his novels, the 1983 *Mr. Palomar* and the 1972 *Invisible Cities,* has his protagonists trying to make the trip from inside, from the interior of consciousness, and in both, attempts to shun the conventional and the facile. The two works are said to be "his most cerebral," *Mr. Palomar* "his most philosophical" (Hume 133).

Invisible Cities, supposedly set in a garden at sunset, purports to be a dialogue between the aging Kublai Khan and the young Venetian traveler Marco Polo. He spends most of his time telling the emperor about the fantastic places he has seen on his expeditions. The first line of the novel sets up a fine tension that remains until the last page: "Kublai Kahn does not necessarily believe everything Marco Polo says" (*Invisible Cities* 5). But the old emperor listens carefully because in the accounts of these cities there is, perhaps, some hope for his troubled realm because he is able to "discern, through the walls and towers destined to crumble, the tracery of a pattern so subtle it could escape the termites' gnawing" (6).

The limitations of language come into play when Polo admits to the Khan, "Every time I describe a city, I am saying something about Venice." The emperor warns him to keep his reportage on track and name the cities, and Polo says, "Memory's images, once they are fixed in words, are erased." This lament over language continues: "Perhaps I am afraid of losing Venice all at once, if I speak of it. Or perhaps, speaking of other cities, I have already lost it, little by little" (86–87).

Mr. Palomar takes place in Palomar's mind, its 27 narratives documenting the fluctuations in his consciousness to everyday sights—the surf, a woman's bare breasts, the mating of tortoises, and his own lawn and garden. His lawn leads him to the heavens, to try to apply his thoughts about the lawn to the universe—"as regular and ordered cosmos or as chaotic proliferation . . . other universes within itself. The universe, collection of celestial bodies, nebulas, fine dust, force fields, intersections of fields, collections of collections" (*Mr. Palomar* 33).

He tries to connect to the planets by contemplating their placement in the firmament and dark space and his own watchful presence (41). What he gains from this, he feels to be precarious, inconsistent—not at all what the ancients could derive from it. He wonders if this is because his relationship with the sky is erratic rather than habitual. Were he an astronomer, tracking the constellations nightly and yearly, perhaps he could gain some understanding of time as something immutable, quite separate from the inconstancy of terrestrial occurrences. Yet, even this might not be enough (47).

Hume proposes that the two novels "might best be likened to space probes, satellites crossing the airless expanses between the everyday world of the visible and the Venus of the self, a bright, beautiful, dangerous, cloud-wrapped and mysterious neighbour." Both, she maintains, "function as fly-bys, not landing craft. Their measurements of the self are indirect, extrapolative, and incomplete . . . this portrait results from oblique glances, not from direct confrontation" (Hume 145).

Polo's expeditions do take on characteristics of fly-bys as *Invisible Cities* progresses, especially when Kublai Kahn questions him, arguing that he hasn't possibly had time to visit all the places he describes and that it seems he's never really left the garden. Polo all but confirms this when he replies: "Everything I see and do assumes meaning in a mental space where the same calm reigns as here, the same penumbra, the same silence streaked by the rustling of leaves." And never is he too far away: "I find myself again, always, in this garden, at this hour of the evening, in your august presence, though I continue, without a moment's pause, moving up a river green with crocodiles or counting the barrels of salted fish being lowered into the hold" (*Invisible Cities* 103).

Kublai Kahn answers, "I, too, am not sure I am here," and Polo suggests: "Perhaps this garden exists only in the shadow of our lowered eyelids, and we have never stopped: you, from raising dust on the fields of battle; and I, from bargaining for sacks of pepper in distant bazaars." And, lending strong support to the fly-by concept, he says, "But each time we half-close our eyes, in the midst of the din and the throng, we are allowed to withdraw here, dressed in silk kimonos, to ponder what we are seeing and living, to draw conclusions, to contemplate from the distance." In this passage, Calvino effects a shift from relative harmony to a state of dissonance when Kublai Kahn says, "Perhaps this dialogue of ours is taking place between two beggars nicknamed Kublai Khan and Marco Polo; as they sift through a rubbish heap, piling up rusted flotsam, scraps of cloth, wastepaper, while drunk on the few sips of bad wine, they see all the treasure of the East shine around them." Polo advances the idea: "Perhaps all that is left of the world is a wasteland covered with rubbish heaps, and the hanging garden of the Great Khan's palace. It is our eyelids that separate them, but we cannot know which is inside and which outside" (103–104).

Bits of trash, fragments whose original purpose is long lost—with these, Calvino carefully lays his groundwork. Polo recalls the city of Moriana's grand face and its hidden, decaying one (105). Likewise, there are two cities of Clarices (106–108), two Eusapias (109–10) and two Beersheebas, one a celestial city of gold with diamond gates and the other located underground, the streets strewn with trash and human leavings. The infernal city is not really separate from the celestial one but a function of it, the whole being "a city which, only when it shits, is not miserly, calculating, greedy" (112–13).

The same disarray is made evident early in *Mr. Palomar,* during Palomar's evening swim when a motorboat speeds by, churning up the surf and sending a big wave to crash on the beach where "the withdrawal of the water now reveals a margin of beach dotted with cans, peanuts, condoms, dead fish, plastic bottles, broken clogs, syringes, twigs black with oil." Mr.
Palomar himself "suddenly feels like flotsam amid flotsam, a corpse rolling on the garbage-beaches of the cemetery-continents" (*Mr. Palomar* 17).

Such debris strongly suggests the chaos of language, and its obverse, the order imposed by silence. Kublai Kahn searches the space surrounding Polo's accounts, "a void not filled with words" (*Invisible Cities* 38). Even though he learns the Kahn's language, words soon fail Polo and he begins "relying on gestures, grimaces, glances." The emperor prefers "a mute commentary, holding up his hands, palms out, or backs, or sideways, in straight or oblique movements, spasmodic or slow." Finally, they communicate in silence (39).

Palomar notes that the courtship of the tortoises is quite a noisy business, but that during the actual mating both are silent. He wonders if the insensitivity of their shells "drives them to a concentrated, intense mental life, leads them to a crystalline inner awareness" ((*Mr. Palomar* 20–21). He had always hoped that "silence contains something more than language can say" (27). He knows too that silence itself can speak, "since it is a rejection of the use to which others put words; but the meaning of this silence-speech lies in its interruptions in what is, from time to time, actually said, giving a meaning to what is unsaid" (103). Palomar has made it a practice to bite his tongue three times before announcing an opinion or handing down a judgment. By the third bite, he is always reminded that being correct or influencing the outcome of something in a positive way means nothing. He can pass weeks and even months saying nothing. "Every time I bite my tongue," he says, "I must think not only of what I am about to say or not say, but also of everything that, whether I say it or do not say it, will be said or not said by me or by others" (102–104). Silence is commentary, silence imposes order.

Hume says that Calvino is not only testing language against silence, but against experience, communication and truth. Finally, he puts it up against death itself (Hume 148).

Palomar, after what he terms "a series of intellectual misadventures not worth recalling" decides to try looking at everything from the outside of himself (*Mr. Palomar* 113). This is unsuccessful. It only leads him back to where he began, and it is here that he assumes his final vantage, observing the world as if he were dead. Doing so, he notes, "is less easy than it might seem. First of all, you must not confuse being dead with not being [because] before birth we are part of the infinite possibilities that may or may not be fulfilled; whereas, once dead, we cannot fulfill ourselves either in the past . . . or in the future" (121–22). Still, the detachment that he has always associated with being dead eludes him (123), and what he finds most difficult to accept is his life being a "closed whole, all in the past, to which you can add nothing" (125). He has an idea that is unprecedented: he will attempt to describe every instant in his existence from this time forward, thereby, he reasons, delaying the end, pushing it further and further away until it is out of sight. But here, at this moment, language inevitably fails him, and he dies (126).

In *Invisible Cities,* Calvino introduces on page 28 the prospect that the Kahn and Polo are of one mind—that is, each part of a double-minded individual. Here, both imagine making the same response. Seventy pages later, their words and actions are "perhaps only imagined, as the two, silent and motionless, watched the smoke rise slowly from their pipes." On page 103, both express the doubt that they are even present in the Khan's garden, and that this is all a dream. On page 118, both agree that *they* do not exist. Does one exist if the other does not? Calvino drops all authorial distance at the end of the novel when he has Polo looking through the Khan's atlas, a special edition which "reveals the form of cities that do not yet have a form or a name," such as the one that "might be called San Francisco" that "spans the Golden Gate and the bay with long, light bridges and sends open trams climbing its steep streets," and that "might blossom as capital of the Pacific a millennium hence, after the long siege of three hundred years that would lead the races of the yellow and the black and the red to fuse with the surviving descendants of the whites in an empire more vast than the Great Khan's." There is another city "in the shape of New Amsterdam known also as New York, crammed with towers of glass and steel on an oblong island between two rivers, with streets like deep canals, all of them straight, except

Broadway." Every shape must find its city, Calvino says, and until then, "new cities will continue to be born" (138–39).

Invisible Cities closes with one last perusal of the atlas and its "maps of the promised lands visited in thought but not yet discovered or founded: New Atlantis, Utopia, the City of the Sun, Oceana, Tamoé, New Harmony, New Lanark, Icaria." The Khan leafs through the volume, "over the maps of the cities that menace in nightmares and maledictions: Enoch, Babylon, Yahooland, Butua, Brave New World" (164). He concludes that the last landing place can only be the infernal city, but Polo disagrees. If there is such a place, he says, it's here now, where we are, what we cause jointly. There are two ways to endure the inferno, he says—either to accept it and to become it or to determine who and what in it are not inferno. They, he says, must be allowed to endure, to be given space (165). The novel ends, just as *Mr. Palomar* closes with the loss of all space.

Calvino, who died in 1985, used a variety of genres and styles, but this fantastical, whimsical fiction is where he excelled. Dillard, discussing Calvino and others, says, "In many works, the world is the arena of possibilities. Anything may happen. This 'anything' is fiction's new subject. Traditional writers labor to make their 'what-ifs' seem plausible. But contemporary modernists flaunt the speculative nature of their fiction. What if, they say, and what if what else?" *Invisible Cities*, she says, "is a wonderful case in point" (58). She sees Calvino's work as "visibly stricken with a sense of a finite material world so long and wide it becomes a material metaphor for infinity" (61).

Is Gardner right—that this is but a nebulous antithesis to Modernism?

A TERMINOLOGICAL FICTION

Barthelme, in his *Paris Review* interview, says that critics are unsure how to deal with Postmodernist fiction, that it is not unprecedented in the history of criticism (O'Hara 209).

Reflecting on 1966–67, Barth says, "[W]e scarcely had the term *Postmodernism* in its current literary-critical usage" but "a number of us, in quite different ways and with varying combinations of intuitive response and conscious deliberation, were already well into the working out, not of the next-best thing after Modernism, but of the *best next* thing: what is gropingly now called Postmodernist fiction" (Barth 121).

Gerald Graff, who believes that the word *postmodernism* has been corrupted, contends that it "should be seen not as a break with romantic and modernist assumptions but rather as a logical culmination of the premises of these earlier movements" (32).

Many commentators maintain that it is Postmodernism's special use of irony that distinguishes it from Modernism. Newman disagrees, arguing that there is an unmistakable link between the two in the ironic *use* of Modernism by certain Postmodernists. He points out that Realism made light of Romance, just as the Bourgeois began to receive ironic treatment in the Bourgeois novel. And now the Postmodernist writer "subjects the Modernists' exclusive emphasis on the protean to parody, ironizing the conventions of fragmentation, simultaneity, and formlessness without end, attacking the dogma of individualized style" (89).

He suggests that Postmodernism "might be understood as a peculiar amalgam of high *and* popular culture, which does not find its place either in habitual adversary or commercial categories, much less in those of Realism and Formalism" (104). And he believes that Postmodernism has "ideologized the epistemological. It mimicks not History but Philosophy" (67). Postmodernism is "the first culture in history totally under the control of 20th century technology, and the first in five hundred years in which information is codified in ways which do not depend on literacy" (186-87).

Still, he says, the Postmodern era, "which began so admirably as the refutation of a sterile continuity, is suffused with the discovery that far from having put Modernism in abeyance, it retains its most salient and questionable features" (202).

Newman calls the word *postmodern* one of many "terminological fictions" with which we must deal, cautioning that "a terminology can have considerable operative power." He calls these "gropings, premonitions and perversions of both language and history," but which "often tell us more about a culture than its highest productions." Therefore, the term *Postmodern* "may in fact mean something beyond its more semantically febrile versions of Art post-partum, post mortem and postponable—a nomenclature which inevitably calls to mind a band of vainglorious contemporary artists following the circus elephants of Modernism with snow shovels" (16–17).

Modernism's "central mythology," he says, tells us that it "was *not* an evolutionary development, but a free radical departure, the evangelical myth of rebirth by fiat" (17). It could be said to have begun "in 1852 as Flaubert writes Louise Colet . . . "The time for Beauty is over. Mankind may return to it, but it has no use for it at present. The more Art develops, the more scientific it will be, just as science will become artistic" (24).

Barth's perspective is similar: "Since 1850 [Modernity] has been our goddess and our demoness. In recent years there has been an attempt to exorcise here, and there has been much talk of 'postmodernism.' But what is postmodernism if not an even more modern modernity?" (298).

"What," he asks, "could be more self-referential than the end of *A Midsummer Night's Dream*, or more effective at representing the denatured human than *Frankenstein*?" (308).

And there is Cervantes:

> Commonly called the first modern novel, *Don Quixote* is in several respects the first postmodern one as well: in its incremental awareness of itself as fiction, in its impassioned and transcendent parody of the genre it ends up glorifying, and not least in its half-ironic amplitude ("My master can go on like this to the end of the

chapter," Sancho Panza remarks of Quixote's effusions). (Barth 87)

Contemporary writing, Newman says (quoted earlier), "exists uneasily between an establishment which sees *Finnegans Wake* as the end of a genre, or a beginning, and an adolescent culture which sees itself as somehow sprung fully armed from the void"(98).

Barth takes this further:

> Was Laurence Sterne's *Tristram Shandy* proto-Modern or proto-Postmodern? More important, was the whole phenomenon, whatever it was, no more than a pallid ghost of the powerful cultural force that international Modernism had been in the first half of this century, or was it a positive new direction in the old art of storytelling, and in other arts as well? Was it a repudiation of the great Modernists at whose figurative feet I had sat, or was it something evolved out of them, some next stage of the ongoing dialectic between artistic generations that has characterized Western Civ at least since the advent of Romanticism in (I'm going to say) the latter eighteenth century? (Barth 119).

Newman says that the word *Postmodern* is seldom found in disciplines lacking a canonical structure susceptible to attack or dismissal: "One does not find it in economics because economists take a more evolutionary view, calling themselves either neo-conservatives or even neo-liberals, and one never sees it in cinematic criticism, where there is no overwhelming sense of history" (22). Since the publication of Newman's book in 1985, however, there have been several films that could be called Postmodern, among them director Sally Potter's 1992 *Orlando*, a just treatment of the Woolf novel, and some of the work of directors Quentin Tarantino and Oliver Stone. The word *postmodern,* Newman says, "pervades art and dance criticism because the specific hegemony of Abstract Expressionism and Balanchine's Neo-classicism are so decisive that Post-Modern becomes a neologism for what one is *not* talking about." In architecture it is used because "Modernism is understood to be a *totally canonized phenomenon;* an indisputable and inescapable monument" (22).

Newman believes that Postmodernism,

> in its positive form constitutes an intellectual attack upon the atomized, passive and indifferent mass culture which, through the saturation of electronic technology, has reached its zenith in Post-War America. The reaction in the 1950's against the falsity and meretriciousness of this culture was expressed through ironic detachment, characterized by a contemplative indifference to politics, the conservation of valued cultural objects in all their complexity, and the missionary spirit associated with late Modernism. (5)

His argument, he insists, is not based on economic determinism, but rather on inflation's being "a cultural malaise of moral dimensions":

> In a little more than a generation, our population has almost doubled, per capita income has increased 1,000%, college enrollment has increased 7 times. Our total gross national product is up more than 2,200%, as is personal spending, as we have undergone an unprecedented global price revolution since WWII of 300-600%, depending on which commodity index is used. The dollar, which was halved in value from 1946-1969, was halved again in the last decade—a trebling of consumer prices reflecting the worst inflation in the history of the Republic. (7)

This "intractable and insidious social phenomenon" (7) has profoundly affected the exchange of ideas (8). In terms of a timeline he would

> periodize Post-Modernism within the velocity of the money supply, which began rising in the spring of 1946, accelerated in the late fifties, peaked in 1969 as the Great Society demanded both a foreign war and a domestic slumber party, continued out of control throughout the seventies, and began to subside only in the summer of 1981, as, one by one, the myths of inflation began to be brutally dismantled. (202)

It ended, he says, "as all aesthetic movements must, when it could provide no values as an alternative to the marketplace—for the mysterious force of all serious art is the extent to which it always exceeds the requirements of the market" (196).

It failed in its mission, he insists, and the term itself "signifies a simultaneous continuity and renunciation, a generation strong enough to dissolve the old order, but too weak to marshal the centrifugal forces it has released. This new literature founders in its own hard won heterogeneity, and tends to lose the sense of itself as a human institution" (5). He says flatly, "there is no such thing as a Post-Modernist canon. Contemporary writers are uniquely different from one another" (12). A look at Postmodernism's forms, which all but defy categorization, bears this out. Postmodernism "harbors the deep suspicion that we have only unpleasant choices; that we may have seen the best civilization has to offer" (61).

Barth puts it in a different light:

> My ideal Postmodernist author neither merely repudiates nor merely imitates either his twentieth-century Modernist parents or his nineteenth-century premodernist grandparents. He has the first half of our century under his belt, but not on his back . . . he nevertheless aspires to a fiction more democratic in its appeal than such late-Modernist marvels as Beckett's *Texts for Nothing*. . . . The ideal Postmodernist novel will somehow rise above the quarrel between realism and irrealism, formalism and "contentism," pure and committed literature, coterie fiction and junk fiction. . . . (120–21)

In North American fiction, he believes that "the pendulum has swung from the overtly self-conscious, process-*and*-history-conscious, and often fabulistic work of Barthelme, Coover, Elkin, Gass, Hawkes, Pynchon, & Co. toward that early-Hemingwayish minimalist neo-realism . . . epitomized by the short stories of Carver, Beattie, Frederick Barthelme . . . and others" (Barth 125).

At this writing in mid-2000, Frederick Barthelme, who has said he does not consider himself a minimalist, had published three short story collection and eight novels. His 1993 *The Brothers*, 1995 *Painted Desert*, and 1997 *Bob the Gambler* could be characterized as accomplished, second-generation Hemingway—the first generation being James Dickey, Harry Crews, and Barry Hannah whose protagonists Light Out for the Territory to Look Death in the Eye. The second generation is equally tough. Their dialogue is guy talk, and their base of operations is within the borders of suburbia. They drive a great deal and consume quantities of mass media with their fries and burgers. Beer is important, especially which upscale brand is appropriate for the occasion. Events pass haphazardly. Danger is capricious. What matters is not the way things are but the way they look, which is what makes second-generation protagonists feel the *stuff*, a good word that captures their haphazard approach to life. There's a sense of drift throughout, which is OK because they're drifters at heart. They're passive, strictly spectators, not confrontational, not inclined to make choices. No one is interested in politics or society or the culture, and if ever they were, they've given up out of hopelessness. They'd rather take a nap or turn on the TV for the latest human catastrophe.

Minimalist neo-realists or *Diet Pepsi minimalists* or *New Postmodernists*, the terms are certain to disappear. By the year 2030, John Barth says, "we won't be calling what we do Postmodernist" and that "2000 seems an appropriate target date for winding up Postmodernism as a cultural and aesthetic dominant, just as 1950 or thereabouts was a historically tidy date for bidding auf Wiedersehen to High Modernism" (Barth 309).

The comic letter that Alphonse writes to Gaston in Donald Barthelme's 1985 essay "Not-Knowing" warrants a last look:

> Dear Gaston
>
> Yes, you are absolutely right—Postmodernism is dead. A stunning blow, but not entirely surprising. I am spreading the news as rapidly as possible, so that all our friends who are in the Postmodernist 'bag' can get out of it before their cars are repossessed and the insurance companies tear up their policies. Sad to see Postmodernism go (and so quickly!). I was fond of it. As fond, almost, as I was of its grave and noble predecessor, Modernism. But we cannot dwell in the done-for. The death of a movement is a natural part of life, as was understood so well by the partisans of Naturalism, which is dead.
>
> I remember exactly where I was when I realized that Postmodernism had bought it. I was in my study with a cup of tequila and William Y's new book, *One-Half*. Y's work is, we agree, good—*very* good. But who can make the leap to greatness while

128

dragging after him the burnt-out boxcars of a dead aesthetic? Perhaps we can find new employment for him. On the roads, for example. When the insight overtook me, I started to my feet, knocking over the tequila, and said aloud (although there was no one to hear), 'What? Postmodernism, too?" So many, so many. I put Y's book away on a high shelf and turned to the contemplation of the death of Plainsong, 958 A.D. (114–15)

Near the letter's end,

What shall we call the New Thing, which I haven't encountered yet but which is bound to be out there somewhere? Post-Postmodernism sounds, to me, a little lumpy. (115)

Following the letter, Barthelme, true to form, clouds the issue: "If I am slightly more sanguine than Alphonse about Postmodernism, however dubious about the term itself and not altogether clear as to whom is supposed to be on the bus and who is not, it's because I locate it in relation to a series of problems, and feel that the problems are durable ones. Problems are a comfort" (115–16).

Eco gets the last word, which serves as introduction to *The Dead Father*:

[W]ith the modern, anyone who does not understand the game can only reject it, but with the postmodern, it is possible not to understand the game and yet to take it seriously. Which is, after all, the quality (the risk) of irony. There is always someone who takes ironic discourse seriously. I think that the collages of Picasso, Juan Gris, and Braque were modern: this is why normal people would not accept them. On the other hand, the collages of Max Ernst, who pasted together pieces of nineteenth-century engravings, were postmodern: they can be read as fantastic stories, as the telling of dreams, without any awareness that they amount to a discussion of the nature of engraving, and perhaps even of collage. If "postmodern" means this, it is clear why Sterne and Rabelais were postmodern, why Borges surely is, and why in the same artist the modern moment and the postmodern moment can coexist, or alternate, or follow each other closely. (68)

WORKS CITED IN THE CHAPTER

Arnason, H. H. *History of Modern Art.* New York: Harry N. Abrams, 1986.

Barth, John. *Further Fridays: Essays, Lectures, and Other Nonfiction 1984–94.* Boston: Little Brown, 1995.

Barthelme, Donald. "Not-Knowing." *Major Writers of Short Fiction: Stories and Commentaries.* Ann Charters, ed. Boston: Bedford Books of St. Martin's Press. 113–24.

Brans, Jo. "Embracing the World: An Interview with Donald Barthelme." *Southwest Review* 67, Spring 1982: 121–37.

Calvino, Italo. *Invisible Cities.* San Diego: Harcourt Brace Jovanovich, 1972.

——. *Mr. Palomar.* San Diego: Harcourt Brace Jovanovich, 1983.

Dillard, Annie. *Living by Fiction.* New York: Harper & Row, 1988.

Eco, Umberto. *Postscript to The Name of the Rose.* San Diego: Harcourt Brace Jovanovich, 1984.

Frye, Northrop. *The Well-Tempered Critic.* Gloucester, MA: Peter Smith, 1963.

Gardner, John. *On Moral Fiction.* New York: Basic Books, 1978.

——. *The Art of Fiction.* New York: Knopf, 1984.

Gass, William H. *Fiction and the Figures of Life*. Boston: David R. Godine, 1979.

Graff, Gerald. *Literature Against Itself: Literary Ideas in Modern Society*. Chicago: U of Chicago P, 1979.

Hume, Kathryn. *Calvino's Fictions: Cogito and Cosmos*. New York: Oxford UP, 1992.

Newman, Charles. *The Post-Modern Aura: The Act of Fiction in an Age of Inflation*. Evanston: Northwestern U P, 1985.

Poole, Gray Johnson. *Architects and Man's Skyline*. New York: Dodd, Mead & Company, 1972.

Trachtenberg, Stanley. *Understanding Donald Barthelme*. Columbia, South Carolina: University of South Carolina Press, 1990.

6 BEST NOVEL: *THE DEAD FATHER*

"Endings are elusive, middles are nowhere to be found, but worst of all is to begin, to begin, to begin," laments the narrator in Donald Barthelme's 1960s story "The Dolt" (*60 Stories* 96).

Barthelme mentions in a 1971 interview that "Perpetua," "Critique de la Vie Quotidienne," "Henrietta and Alexandra," and "Flying to America" were "parts of a novel which failed. . . . They may be thought of as the neck, wings, and drumsticks of a turkey" (Klinkowitz 49). In the same conversation: "I am always working on a novel. But they always seem to fall apart in my hands. I still have hopes, however" (51).

John Barth recalls: "Knowing that Donald's novels did not come to him as naturally as his short stories, I once very tentatively asked him, in the period of his wrestling with *The Dead Father,* how that project was coming along. 'Oh, it's finished,' he replied. 'Now all I have to do is *write* the damn thing'" (91).

With publication of the novel in 1975 came intense critical responses. In the *New York Times Book Review,* Roger Shattuck wrote that the novel "presents itself on a larger scale, really as cryptic allegory. But it lacks any sense of jeopardy and urgency. We learn very early that it is all cardboard" (50). In the *Yale Review* Maureen Howard said, "This cold short narrative is written at an extreme distance from life, out of literary models and the author's idea of a defunct avant-garde" (408).

These complaints and others, however, are merely targeting the absence of conventional realism and firing a broadside against Postmodernist writing in general. Gardner charges that "even at his best, as in *The Dead Father*, Barthelme goes not for the profound but for the clever" (81).

The jackdaw again.

'DEAD BUT STILL WITH US'

Some of the artistic choices made in *The Dead Father* are clever, but they serve the whole novel. And it does succeed in what Barthelme always claimed he sought: "a meditation upon external reality" (Brans 123), "a meditation about the world" (Roe 108). Bewailing cleverness in this novel is inevitable since, for starters, the Dead Father is still alive and kicking. But his children are not joking when they call him "an old fart" (10)—one who has outlived his usefulness—and "a motherfucker" (76)—one impossible to live with. At the end of the italicized prologue's three-quarter-page opening paragraph is the narrator's statement: "*Dead, but still with us, still with us, but dead*" (3). This is followed by: "*We want the Dead Father to be dead. We sit with tears in our eyes wanting the Dead Father to be dead—meanwhile doing amazing things with our hands*" (5). He has become obsolete, and it is time for the children to take over.

The opening lines of the prologue begin a detailed description of the father, a colossus toppled to earth:

> The Dead Father's head. The main thing is, his eyes are open. Staring up into the sky. The eyes a two-valued blue, the blues of the Gitanes cigarette pack. The head never moves. Decades of staring. The brow is noble, good Christ, what else? Broad and noble. And serene, of course, he's dead, what else if not serene? From the tip of his finely shaped delicately nostriled nose to the ground, fall of five and one half meters, figure obtained by triangulation. (3)

He is being pulled by 19 men to a trench where he will be covered by bulldozers. But he's not Gulliver come to Lilliput.

> No one can remember when he was not here in our city, positioned like a sleeper in troubled sleep, the whole great expanse of him running from the Avenue Pommard to the Boulevard Grist. Overall length, 3,200 cubits. Half buried in the ground, half not.

work ceaselessly night and day through all the hours for the good of all. He controls the hussars. Controls the rise, fall, and flutter of the market. Controls what Thomas is thinking, what Thomas has always thought, what Thomas will ever think, with exceptions. (3–4)

As to his age, "Maybe a hundred," someone says, he replies, "Wrong, but close. Even older than that, but also younger. Having it both ways is a thing I like" (15). Double there, multiple elsewhere. In his lifetime he has fathered

> the poker chip, the cash register, the juice extractor, the kazoo, the rubber pretzel, the cuckoo clock, the key chain, the dime bank, the pantograph, the bubble pipe, the punching bag both light and heavy, the inkblot, the nose drop, the midget Bible, the slot-machine slug, and many other useful and humane cultural artifacts, as well as some thousands of children of the ordinary sort. I fathered as well upon her various institutions useful and humane such as the credit union, the dog pound, and parapsychology. I fathered as well various realms and territories all superior in terrain, climatology, laws and customs to this one. I overdid it but I was madly, madly in love, that is all I can say in my own defense. It was a very creative period but my darling, having mothered all this abundance uncomplainingly and without reproach, at last died of it. In my arms of course. Her last words were "enough is enough, Pappy." (36)

In addition, he produced a Savings & Loan Association: "Six and three quarters percent compounded momentarily, said the Dead Father. I guarantee it" (38).

But he's equally destructive. In anger over being excluded from sex with Julie, the central female of the novel, he escapes to a grove where he slays a large number of musicians. The description of the kinds of musicians is extravagant: "a blower upon the marrow trumpet and one upon the slide trumpet and one who wearing upon his head the skin of a cat performed upon the menacing cornu and three blowers on the hunting horn" (11). This covers the better part of a page, and whenever one of these catalogs appears in Barthelme's work, it's usually foregrounding, setting up something. In this case, it's the trivialization of his feat by Julie. He plants his sword "in the red and steaming earth," then "pulled from his trousers his ancient prick and pissed upon the dead artists, severally and together, to the best of his ability—four minutes, or one pint."

Julie calls his achievement "Impressive. . . had they not been pure cardboard" (11–12).

She asks him, "[D]id you ever want to paint or draw or etch?" and he replies that it was unnecessary "because I am the Father. All lines my lines. All figure and all ground mine, out of my head. All colors mine. You take my meaning." In the next paragraph: "We had no choice, said Julie (18–19).

Just who is the Dead Father? Some of the novel's favorable reviews attempt to resolve the mystery. "He is God first of all," says Richard Todd, writing in the *Atlantic*, who goes on to tell us that after God, the Dead Father can be whatever we want: "The novel, Western Culture, Truth, Duty, Honor, Country. He is the order that we seek, and the control we seek to escape" (112).

The Dead Father isn't God but *godlike*, and Todd's last sentence is close to the mark, especially in tandem with Neil Schmitz's comments in *Partisan Review*: "[T]he Dead Father is finally everyone's father, the great mutilated self-important, self-indulgent Super-ego whom we pull along behind us" (306). In the novel, the Dead Father says, "Without children I would not be the Father. No Fatherhood without childhood." But unrelentingly authoritarian, he makes sure that his male progeny always wear cap-and-bells (17).

Barthelme's own comment, though less than lucid, is the answer: "*The Dead Father* suggests that the process of becoming has bound up in it the experience of many other consciousnesses, the most important of which are in a law-giving relation to the self" (O'Hara 201). All through the novel are attributes associated with omnipotence, but rather than of divine origin, they're a projection of the mortal.

Davis sums up the opening lines—"The details of his features soon make it apparent that his different parts are emblems of paternity and that this character is to be taken as a complex symbol"—and considers the description: "His noble brow stands for mental power and concentration. His rugged jawline indicates formidable will and endurance. His blue eyes and gray hair show his attractive and even dashing appearance" (186).

In the novel: "The father's voice is an instrument of the most terrible pertinaciousness" (123).

And, three pages back is good reason to fear the voice:

> The best way to approach a father is from behind. Thus if he chooses to hurl his javelin at you, he will probably miss. For in the act of twisting his body around, and drawing back his hurling arm, and sighting along the shaft, he will give you time to run, to make reservations for a flight to another country. (120)

O'Hara observes that the novel crosses the border "into Kafka country," and suggests to Barthelme that "God has shown himself to be a bad father. But you seem not to believe in God, whereas Kafka did." To this, Barthelme answers: "Well, actually the Holy Ghost is my main man, as we say" (201) This statement brings to mind Ihab Hassan, setting down Postmodernism's "certain schematic differences from modernism": he lists "The Holy Ghost" under the Postmodern, and "God the Father" under Modern (Hassan 592).

Barthelme tells O'Hara: "I don't think I've ever had much to say about God except as a locus of complaint, a convention, someone to rail against" (O'Hara 201).

The germinating idea for this novel, Barthelme reveals in another interview, was "[a] matter of having a father and being a father." To the statement "In some basic sense the book deals with the notion that we're all dragging around behind us the corpses of our fathers, as well as the past in general," he responds: "Worse: dragging these *ahead* of us" (McCaffrey 41).

Alluding to parallels between *The Dead Father* and Beckett's *Molloy*,[17] O'Hara asks him if he shares the sense that "Beckett's pronouncements on art

---

[17] *Molloy* is more concerned with metaphysical matters, *The Dead Father* with relationships.

imply something curious: that artists who in the past assumed and sought to convey ultimate truths (as Dante did) were quite right, but that in our own time these truths don't exist and therefore the artist must proceed differently." Barthelme quotes Beckett, saying that he "rejects what can be accomplished 'on the plane of the feasible'—he seems to be asking for an art adequate to the intuition of Nothingness." The job to be done—"the problem" he calls it— "appears to be not one of announcing truths, or that truths do or do not exist, but of hewing to the intuition, which seems central, and yet getting some work done." Barthelme calls Beckett's work "an embarrassment to the Void," and invokes the German writer Heimito von Doderer as explanation: "'At first you break windows. Then you become a window yourself'" (O'Hara 202). And so it is with fathers in art.

Davis calls *The Dead Father* "possibly the most important 'father' novel since *Ulysses* and *Absalom, Absalom!*" and that the "complex and brilliant work accomplishes nothing less than a major redefinition of what the father in fiction is, and it does this as it forces novelistic attention to range back, over the structure of the father in English fiction" (185)

In the opening description of the Dead Father's head, Davis sees a rogues' gallery of fathers, those who are strict but kindhearted, including Squire Allworthy, John Jarndyce, Edward Overton. There are saintly figures such as those John Bunyan's Christian encountered in the Celestial City. And at the far end of the gallery are those who hate children, Mr. Murdstone, Mr. M'Choakumchild, Sir Austen Feverel, Huck Finn's Pap, and Thomas Sutpen, and, beyond them the killers of children, Wash Jones, Percy Grimm, and others. Barthelme's Dead Father is all of these, Davis believes, and it's risky business: "A fiction that taps this tradition by daring to seize the father as a whole stands in peril of some presumption, as does the attempt to understand that fiction" (185–86).

Despite its being a Postmodern novel, he says, *The Dead Father* is "part of an English tradition of fiction (*Robinson Crusoe, The Ordeal of Richard Feverel*, etc.) that explicitly articulates the function of paternity both thematically and structurally" and "must still deal with the residue of father images, mostly social and economic in origin, that belong to the English tradition of realistic fiction." This brings to mind, he says, "the portrait of a mature gentleman in a suit with vest, with graying hair and glasses and perhaps a watch chain slung across his middle. He is Squire Allworthy, Sir Austen Feverel, Edward Overton, or Jason Lycurgus Compson, III—a composite of the rogues' gallery figures" (187).

The novel makes use of traditional structures, Davis says. The Dead Father is seen performing heroic deeds in his quest for the Golden Fleece with which he hopes to renew himself. This "links Barthelme's novel to *Robinson Crusoe, Huckleberry Finn, Moby Dick, Ulysses*, and many others." Another quest convention is apparent, he says, when "as the journey's end nears a female (her name is "Mother") is liberated, her entrance into the action obviously connected with the consummation of the journey." Besides the quest, he says, "there is the highly traditional novelistic device of the book-within-a-book. The novel's 'A Manual for Sons' gives practical guidance, in the manner of a field manual, for identifying and dealing with what it calls the important nineteen of the twenty-two possible kinds of fathers." These conventional devices, the quest and book-within-a-book, Davis says, "create a picture, and an accurate one, of a novel solidly ensconced in the English tradition." And irony comes in because the quest actually "casts suspicion on the status of its quester: he is at times comatose and at other times frenetic." No woman is willing to participate with him in sex, and he is always restrained in his advances by Thomas who raps him sharply on the head (187–88).

The Dead Father follows a path familiar in literature, Davis says. "This novel's manner of signifying the father structurally belongs to tradition: like the fathers in *Robinson Crusoe, Tom Jones,* and *Huckleberry Finn* the father must be lost so that, in his absence, his function can be known." In terms of structure, "it is father absence, not presence, that signifies the father: the father is lost so that his meaning can be found symbolically. At the same time, the manner in which the father is presented here is not a mere repetition." Davis's view is that "Barthelme draws his paternal material from the rogues' gallery of traditional images, compresses it into a single image of the father, then allows that image to fall like a straw man, leaving the locus of the father in its place." By doing so, *The Dead Father* "uses the material of the realistic novel to advance beyond the realistic novel and is at once thoroughly traditional and post-modern." If the novel were "truly satiric or parodic," it would be oriented "toward a merely traditional depiction of the father," but done the way it is, "this fiction employs irony to undermine its own materials in order to signify the father anew" (194).

Barthelme, then, is doing a two-step here, "simultaneously a representation of the rogues' gallery of fathers (the whole of the paternal tradition) and a denial of paternity," the result being that "the Dead Father's character comprises a fiction at a high level of abstraction. A fiction dealing in these cerebral strokes—the whole of the paternal tradition in fiction is evoked and then desiccated—verges on defining itself more as criticism than as fiction." Again, not without risk, because "to posit fiction at this level of abstraction is to gamble reader engagement on very thin odds: character, plot, theme, setting, and symbolism—all are tossed into a sea of abstraction that only specialized knowledge (a critical awareness) of the English tradition and its underlying structures can navigate" (194).

Warnings like these have been heard before, he says, "about *Ulysses* and *Finnegans Wake*, about Faulkner's novels, and about many others; with Joyce and Faulkner, readers have come into being because their novels needed reading— they were too important to be left unread."

But relatively few have read those books through, and Barthelme's chances are worse, because like Joyce with the *Wake*, he's asking so much of the reader:

> The special boldness (and danger) of Barthelme's fiction is that it flirts with surface nonsense, as does much fiction by William Gass, Thomas Pynchon, John Barth, Hunter Thompson, and Tom Robbins. This flirtation creates the appearance of peripatetic elements (the name "Oedipa Maas" in *The Crying of Lot 49* is a good example) that are methodically drained of their significance, so that the father—as a principle of order—is continually promised, but his articulation is deferred, sometimes indefinitely. This narrative technique, an apparent abnegation of the father, can be deciphered as fictional sense only at another level very far removed from the play of images and from what is commonly known as texture—elements that traditionally convey the pleasure of the text for readers. (194)

In *The Dead Father,* Davis says, Barthelme

> wagers the ancient bet that the father may be seized in his totality, directly: it tries to grasp his essential shape—in effect, to break through his pasteboard mask. This ambitious striving, a strike against tradition, necessarily requires a sacrifice of pleasure, one that Barthelme boldly makes. That the bet is lost and the father not seized are foregone conclusions; that loss is as much a part of the ritual of fiction-making as is the need to take such risks. Paradoxically, it is in that necessary "failure" at the level of narrative structure, wherein the father is not seized in his totality, that the novel signifies most directly the paternal symbol it cannot possess. (195).

THREE IRONIES

Davis identifies three major ironies of the novel, the first being the traditional quest—or the notion of one. The second is the role of the female, notably the revelation of the identity of the "horseman on the hill" (32) in the closing pages of the novel (170). Davis says, "Mother's appearance at the end reflects a pattern of feminine experience that does not belong in the traditional masculine cast of the quest" (189). As she approaches on horseback, Thomas recognizes her and immediately proceeds to give her a grocery list of 26 items, ranging from Fig Newtons to tennis balls. He thanks her and she rides away. The Dead Father says, "I don't remember her very

well. . . . What was her name?" (*Dead Father* 169–70).

Davis connects this to two of the other female characters in the novel.

> And not only is Mother foreign to him; his daughters Julie and Emma he sees only as possibilities for sexual conquest and is virtually unable to communicate with them. Were the Dead Father to attempt to talk to them, he would find that they, while speaking English, have a language of their own. Instead of the Germanic assertion-question-response pattern of English conversation, Julie and Emma speak a language of free association mixed with guardedly private connotations—a language of the oppressed. (188–89)

The first of these, an exchange between Julie and Emma, occurs early in the novel when Julie approaches Emma and asks her,

> Whose little girl are you?
> I get by, I get by.
> Time to go.
> Hoping this will reach you at a favorable moment.
> Bad things can happen to people.
> Is that a threat?
> Dragged him all this distance without any rootytoottoot.
> Is that a threat?
> Take it any way you like it. (23)

Davis sees parallels between "their oblique communication and Mother's roundabout way of traveling," both of which "suggest an a-linear model of behavior foreign to the rational economies associated with paternal authority." The Mother's distancing of herself from the Dead Father's procession and the apparent aimlessness of Julie and Emma's dialogue deviate "perversely from the predictable path of formal discourse. As if not dependent on the stringencies of verbal exchange, they communicate through what is unstated but recognized as mutual experience. They do reach a destination in their conversation, but the route they take cannot be known in advance" (189).

Barthelme's own explanation: "The dialogues in *The Dead Father* are really collections of non sequiturs, intended to give the novel another kind of voice, to provide a kind of counter-narration to the main narration. Then I got interested in doing them for their own sake, with a little more narrative introduced."(Brans 134). In another interview he also discusses these "four or five passages in which the two principal women talk to each other, or talk *against* each other, or over each other's heads, or between each other's legs—passages which were possible because there is a fairly strong narrative line surrounding them."

In later work, we see trials of dialogues with varying amounts of narrative. "It's a question as to whether such things can be made to fly without support of a controlling narrative. As, for example, in the final story of *Great Days* which is, I think, more or less successful" (McCaffrey 41–42). This was "The Leap," the last piece in the 1979 *Great Days* collection.

As in "The Leap" and others, the dialogues between Julie and Emma are collages, barely connected to adjacent lines and surrounding narrative or not at all. In the section above, Julie's hostility to Emma is apparent, and in subsequent lines, Emma shows attraction to Thomas. There are repeated lines throughout the novel, and their relevance to the context varies—"Pop one of these if you'd like a little lift" (23, 25, 27, 154), "Hoping this will reach you at a favorable moment" (23, 24, 86, 155), "I can make it hot for you" (24, 25, 26, 61, 150). The line "Thought I heard a dog barking" (25, twice on 26, 62, 86, 148) probably refers to the Mother, who is trailing the procession on horseback almost to the end of the novel. But regarding Barthelme's statement that these "non sequiturs" furnish a "counter-narration," they appear to lack the coherence to do so.

On the other hand, as Walsh suggests, these dialogues, in "their refusal of the dictates of meaning," could be seen as a "model of fatherlessness, of nonpatriarchal society: an anarchist-feminist enclave within the narrative of the expedition." Emma's function in the novel is "as a foil to Julie, who is established throughout the book as the antithesis of the Dead Father and the principal advocate of the chaos of fatherlessness that Thomas must balance against the Dead Father's authority." Their dialogues, then, "offer, as narrative mode, an alternative to the Dead Father as origin of meaning. As such they stand in parallel with the other models of fatherlessness that are offered in the course of the expedition, all of which prove inadequate" (179).

The first of these appears early in the novel, two children, a male and a female: "Children in love, said Julie." She knows this because "I have an eye for love." The Dead Father calls them "Whippersnappers." The children ask what he is, and Thomas tells them.

> The children hugged each other tightly.
> He doesn't look dead to us, said the girl.
> He is walking, said the boy. Or standing up, anyhow.
> He is dead only in a sense, Thomas said.
> The children kissed each other, on the lips.
> They don't seem very impressed, said the Dead Father. Where is the awe?
> They are lost in each other, said Julie. Soaks up all available awe. (14)

Walsh calls "[t]heir attitude toward the Dead Father . . . a naïve-utopian freedom from the thrall of his authority" (179).

Thomas asks how old they are.

> We are twenty, said the girl. I am ten and he is ten. Old enough. We are going to live together all our lives and love each other all our lives until we die. We know it. But don't tell anyone because we'll be beaten, if the knowledge becomes general. (14)

This, Walsh explains, "is an inadequate model because it is utterly private, unable to survive exposure to society at large" (179).

The second model of a society that claims to be free of paternity is that of the Wends, encountered by the procession at a roadblock on the border of Wend country. The Wend chieftain explains:

> We Wends are not like other people. We Wends are the fathers of ourselves.
> You are?
> Yes, said the Wend, that which all men have wished to be, from the very beginning, we are.
> Amazing, said Thomas, how is that accomplished?
> It is accomplished by being a Wend, the leader said. Wends have no wives, they have only mothers. Each Wend impregnates his own mother and thus fathers himself. We are all married to our mothers, in proper legal fashion.
> Thomas was counting on his fingers.
> You are skeptical, said the chief. That is because you are not a Wend.
> The mechanics of the thing elude me, said Thomas.
> Take my word for it, said the Wend, it is not more difficult than Christianity. . . . (*Dead Father* 73).

The novel's third major irony, according to Davis, is the status of Thomas as he heads this mission, not only to inter the Dead Father but to bring about a transfer of authority. Thomas, the apparent heir, would become Father, imposing the wearing of cap-and-bells on others. Thomas, however, is passive, a stutterer, a failure at many of his endeavors. But, as Davis points out, "he can sustain himself with very limited successes." In recounting these, Thomas "implies that his strength is to be found in his failures, as the first requirement of one who would become the father is that he is willing to undergo preparation, that is, to be a son, who by definition is in a passive or subservient position" (189).

One night, around the campfire, with "cats crying in the distance," the Dead Father asks Thomas to tell him a story.

Thomas agrees, and without once stuttering relates a surreal, "Paraguay"-like trek to Elsewhere. He is kidnapped by "four men in dark suits" with "attaché cases containing Uzi submachine guns"; the men tell him that he "was wrong and had always been wrong and would always be wrong" (*Dead Father* 40). They travel by horse, Land-Rover, and pirogue to a specific destination (40–42): "We were going to see the Great Father Serpent, they said, the Great Father Serpent would if I answered the riddle correctly grant me a boon but it was one boon to a customer and I would never answer the riddle correctly so my hopes, they said, should not be got up" (43).

At last, Thomas hears a distant clamor that he knows is significant. "The roaring they told me was the voice of the Great Father Serpent calling for the foreskins for the uninitiated but I was safe, my foreskin had been surrendered long ago, to a surgeon in a hospital" (44).

All this is unusually Symbolist for Barthelme. And Joycean: "As we drew near through the tangling vines I perceived the outlines of a serpent of huge bigness which held in its mouth a sheet of tin on which something was written, the roars rattled the tin and I was unable to make out the message" (44).

On the tin is written the answer to the riddle, and by chance Thomas sees it while the Great Father Serpent is being dressed for the riddling, first in "fine smallclothes of softwhispering blushcolored changeable taffeta," to which is added "a kind of scarlet skirt stuffed with bombast and pleated and slashed so as to show a rich inner lining of a lighter scarlet, the two scarlets together making a brave show at his slightest movement or undulation"; and then "they covered the upper or more headward length of him with a light jacket of white silk embroidered with a thread nutmeg in color and a thread goose-turd in color, these intertwined, and trimmed with fine whipped lace." More than a page is devoted to this step-by-step attiring—a doublet, a great cloak, a girdle, and a French hat (44–45)—of the Great Father Serpent, who can only be Joyce.

Nodding once at his image in the sheet of tin, he "pronounced himself ready to riddle":

> Here is the riddle said the Great Father Serpent with a great flourishing of his two-tipped tongue, and it is a son-of-a-bitch I will tell you that, the most arcane item in the arcana, you will never guess it in a hundred thousand human years some of which I point out have already been used up by you in useless living and

breathing but have a go, have a go, do: *What do you really feel?*
(45–46)

Thomas answers, "Like murderinging," not because he'd ever felt it but because he'd seen it on the sheet of tin, "the wording *murderinging* inscribed in a fine thin cursive." The Great Father Serpent and Thomas's abductors could not be more surprised. Thomas is too. "I myself wondered, and marveled, but what I was wondering and marveling at was the closeness with which what I had answered accorded with my feelings, my lost feelings that I had never found before." The Great Father Serpent grants the boon, adding, "but may I remind you that having the power is often enough. You don't have to actually do it. For the soul's ease" (46).

The Dead Father realizes the implications of what he has just heard. Thomas finishes the story:

> I thanked the Great Father Serpent; he bowed most cordially; my companions returned me to the city. I was abroad in the city with murderinging in mind—the dream of a stutterer.
> That is a tall tale, said the Dead Father. I don't believe it ever happened.
> No tale ever happened in the way we tell it, said Thomas, but the moral is always correct.
> What is the moral?
> Murderinging, Thomas said.
> Murderinging is not correct, said the Dead Father. The sacred and noble Father should not be murdereded. Never. Absolutely not.
> I mentioned no names, said Thomas. (46)

Davis says the story reveals the strength concealed within Thomas's passivity, that beneath "the facade of an obedient son, Thomas finds that he is a murderer":

> In the initiation rite, an exercise in creative passivity, Thomas taps the "lost feelings that I had never found before" and acknowledges guilt for a primal crime that he has no distinct memory of committing. Yet the admission of a murderous desire makes it unnecessary for him to murder: by accepting guilt for a

crime that has already taken place, Thomas need not perform the act he has acknowledged responsibility for. In effect, because Thomas identifies the source of his aggressivity, he need not play out aggression by killing fathers. This admission, and the ability to accept guilt and limitation that it implies, place him in line for the Dead Father's authority (190).

Because of this, the Dead Father has now lost ground, and Thomas is able to take from him his silver buckle, marking the first of the symbolic transfers of power. The Father's sword will follow, then his passport and keys.

Walsh says:

> The shape of the novel is determined by Thomas's efforts to complete the transfer of power without in the process becoming the image of the Dead Father, the crucial issue being whether it is possible to usurp the Dead Father's position without also taking on his monolithic perspective. The balance is very fine between transformation and repetition in Thomas's appropriation to himself of the role of father; he is seduced by some of its rewards, notably the pleasure of control, into a dangerous proximity with the position represented by the Dead Father. The significant difference, however, is that when confronted Thomas does not attempt a mystification of the role of fatherhood but frankly confesses its attractions, while the Dead Father's preferred policy is an obfuscation of the nature of power relations. (181)

Thomas is given a book, "a frayed tattered disintegrating volume with showers of ratsnest falling out of it" (*Dead Father* 108), entitled "A Manual for Sons." The Manual gives advice on a father-son relationship that reinforces the many of the attributes seen in the Dead Father—his authoritarianism, his rule-giving, his appetites for women, his treatment of them.

> Fathers are like blocks of marble, giant cubes, highly polished, with veins and seams, placed squarely in your path. They block your path. They cannot be climbed over, neither can they be slithered past. They are the "past," and very likely the slither, if the slither is thought of as that accommodating maneuver you make to escape notice, or get by unscathed. If you attempt to go around one, you will find that another (winking at the first) has

mysteriously appeared athwart the trail. Or maybe it is the same one, moving with the speed of paternity. (129)

Julie articulates this earlier in the book in what she describes as a digression but which accurately characterizes the paternal functions:

> The fucked mother conceives, Julie said. The whelpling is, after agonies I shall not describe, whelped. Then the dialogue begins. The father speaks to it. The "it" in a paroxysm of not understanding. The "it" whirling as in a centrifuge. Looking for something to tie to. Like a boat in a storm. What is there? The father.
> Where is the mother? asked Emma.
> The mother hath not the postlike quality of the father. She is more like a grime.
> A grime?
> Overall presence distributed in discrete small black particles all over everything, said Julie.
> Post and grime, said the Dead Father. You do have a dismal view of things. (77)

Davis elaborates, seeing the father as "the one who intrudes in the child's free state and also to be the primary object in relation to which the child is established in the world. That is, as the child's first intruder who blocks continuance in the 'storm,' the father presents a solution to a dilemma he himself creates for the child (190–91).

The Manual also advances the argument of the novel as regards the transfer of paternal power to the son. It closes on the subjects and death and patricide.

On death:

> Transfers of power of this kind are marked with appropriate ceremonies; top hats are burned. Fatherless now, you must deal with the memory of a father. Often that memory is more potent than the living presence of a father, is an inner voice commanding, haranguing, yes-ing and no-ing—a binary code, yes no yes no yes no yes no, governing your every, your slightest movement, mental or physical. At what point do you become yourself? Never, wholly,

you are always partly him. That privileged position in your inner ear is his last "perk" and no father has ever passed it by. (144)

Patricide is discouraged by the Manual:

It is all right to feel this hot emotion, but not to act upon it. And it is not necessary. It is not necessary to slay your father, time will slay him, that is a virtual certainty. Your true task lies elsewhere.

Your true task, as a son, is to reproduce every one of the enormities touched upon in this manual, but in attenuated form. You must become your father, but a paler, weaker version of him. The enormities go with the job, but close study will allow you to perform the job less well than it has previously been done, thus moving toward a golden age of decency, quiet, and calmed fevers. Your contribution will not be a small one, but "small" is one of the concepts that you should shoot for. (145)

Davis believes the Manual "tells plainly what the rest of the novel suggests all along: the father's authority is not a social force—expressed by privileged males who perform particular acts in the world—but a function within the structure of the mind that can be depicted only symbolically" (192). This is confirmed in the next-to-last chapter of *The Dead Father* where "endshrouded in endigmas" (172) is a key phrase. Davis explains: "The primary "endigma," then, that this novel points to, is the meaning of the Dead Father—a figure the novel presents simultaneously as a character in a fiction and as a symbolic function" (192).

Just prior to reaching the excavation where the bulldozers wait on the other side of a hill, there is a Joycean interior monologue by the Dead Father. As Davis says, it is "Molly Bloom-like" (193), but even more it's *Finnegan*-like in look and feel: "AndI. EndI. Great endifarce teeterteeterteetertottering. Willit urt. I reiterate. Don't be cenacle. Conscientia mille testes. And having made them, where now? what now?" (171).

He was once like them, all his children: "[L]ist, list,[18] let's go back. To the wetbedding. To the dampdream. AndI a oneohsevenyearold boy, just like the rest of them. Pitterpatter. I reiterate&reinterate&reiterate&reiterate, pitterpatter" (171). He recalls when 44 maidens "came to my couch that eve all lovely and giddygay and roaratorious and tumtickling AndI paprikaed many papooses that night. I the All-Father but I never figured out figured out wot sort of animal AndI was. Endshrouded in endigmas. Never knew wot's wot" (172). That some readers find this admission compelling is one measure of the novel's success.

He finishes with a plea that the children not "undertake the OldPap yet. Let's have a party. Pap in on a few old friends. Pass the papcorn. Wield my pappenheimer once again. Old Angurvadal! Companion of my finest hours!"

Now comes another admission: "Thegreatestgoodofthegreatestnumber was a Princeapple of mine. I was compassionate, insofarasitwaspossibleto-beso. Best I cud I did! Absolutely! No dubitatio about it! Don't like! Don't want! Pitterpatter oh please pitterpatter" (173); and here, the monologue ends, without a period.

The *Finnegans Wake* closing comes to mind, Anna Livia's dream monologue where, swept along by water, she makes a stirring reference to her father: "Carry me along, taddy, like you done through the toy fair!" (Joyce 628).

Barthelme's final chapter is as close to Hemingway as anything he ever wrote—tension in voices as Death is stared down, dignity, and of course those silences:

> They straggled up the edge of the excavation.
> Who has dug this great hole in the ground? asked the Dead Father. What is to be builded here?
> Nothing, Thomas said.
> How long it is, the Dead Father observed.
> Long enough, said Thomas, I think.
> The Dead Father looked again at the hole.
> Oh, he said, I see. (174)

---

[18] *Hamlet* I.v.22, the Ghost: "List, list, O, list! / If thou didst ever thy dear father love. . . . Revenge his foul and most unnatural murder."

However disinclined he may be, he must recline.

> No more after this?
> Don't believe so, said Thomas, can I help you off with the loop?
> Together they maneuvered the loop from the Dead Father's torso.
> I wasn't really fooled, said the Dead Father. Not for a moment. I knew all along.
> We knew you knew, said Thomas.
> Of course I had hopes, said the Dead Father. Pale hopes.
> We knew that too.
> Did I do it well? asked the Dead Father.
> Marvelously well, said Julie. Superbly. I will never see it done better.
> Thank you, said the Dead Father. Thank you very much. (176)

Robertson, arguing that much of Barthelme's work can "enact the proposition that language speaks us rather than the other way around," goes on to say that his "focus on language as both symptom and source of mental, spiritual, and social incoherence links him to Hemingway, who, by Barthelme's own admission, had the strongest influence on him." It is not only minimalism, she insists, but an acceptance of Hemingway's basic assumption that our words have been worn out from misuse:

> Hemingway still thought it was possible to locate a few words that were "real," and he used them magisterially. He still thought there was a language of nature that was authentic. In Barthelme that nature is nowhere to be found, and he shows that the very notion of "real" words is naive now, if it wasn't always so. Yet one never feels that he has just abandoned Hemingway's concern for authentic speech as other "fabulators" have—"authentic" meaning some necessary correlation between speech and fact. (Robertson 127)

WORKS CITED IN THE CHAPTER

Barth, John. *Further Fridays: Essays, Lectures, and Other Nonfiction 1984–94.* Boston: Little Brown, 1995.

Barthelme, Donald. *The Dead Father.* New York: Penguin, 1986.

——. *60 Stories.* New York: Penguin, 1993.

Brans, Jo. "Embracing the World: An Interview with Donald Barthelme." *Southwest Review* 67, Spring 1982: 121–37.

Davis, Robert Con. "Post-Modern Paternity: Donald Barthelme's *The Dead Father.*" *Critical Essays on Donald Barthelme.* Ed. Richard F. Patteson. New York: G. K. Hall (Macmillan), 1992.

Gardner, John. *On Moral Fiction.* New York: Basic Books, 1978.

Howard, Maureen. "Recent Novels: A Backward Glance." *Yale Review* 65 (1976): 408.

Hassan, Ihab. "Toward a Concept of Postmodernism." *Postmodern American Fiction: A Norton Anthology.* Ed. Paula Geyh, Fred G. Leebron, and Andrew Levy. New York: Norton, 1998. 586–95.

Joyce, James. *Finnegans Wake.* New York: Penguin, 1976.

Klinkowitz, Jerome. "Donald Barthelme." *The New Fiction: Interviews with Innovative American Writers.* Ed. Joe David Bellamy. Urbana: U of Illinois P, 1974. 45–54.

O'Hara, J. D. "Donald Barthelme: The Art of Fiction LXVI." *Paris Review* 80 (1981): 180–210.

Robertson, Mary. "Postmodern Realism: Discourse As Antihero in Donald Barthelme's "Brain Damage." *Critical Essays on Donald Barthelme.* Ed. Richard F. Patteson. New York: G. K. Hall (Macmillan), 1992.

Roe, Barbara. *Donald Barthelme: A Study of the Short Fiction.* New York: Twayne, 1992.

Schmitz, Neil. "Barthelme's Life with Father." *Partisan Review* 46 (1979): 306.

Shattuck, Roger. *"The Dead Father."* *New York Times Book Review.* 9 November 1975: 50.

Todd, Richard. "Daddy, You're Perfectly Swell!" *Atlantic* 236 (December 1975): 112.

Walsh, Richard. *"The Dead Father:* Innovative Forms, Eternal Themes." *Critical Essays on Donald Barthelme.* Richard F. Patteson, ed. New York: G. K. Hall (Macmillan), 1992.

7 THE SWAN SONGS

The final entries in the chronology appended to Barbara Roe's study of Donald Barthelme's short fiction are:

> 1986 Publishes *Paradise*, a novel; program chair for 48th International PEN Congress in New York City.
>
> 1987 Publishes *Forty Stories*, chiefly selections from earlier books, and *Sam's Bar: An American Landscape*, a picture-text collaboration by mail and telephone with Seymour Chwast.
>
> 1988 Diagnosed with throat cancer; given favorable prognosis after both surgery and chemotherapy; participates with Fiedler, Hawkes, and Coover in Brown University conference on postmodernism; receives Prix de Rome.
>
> 1989 "Tickets," last story in *New Yorker*, appears 6 March; in June, returns ill from American Academy in Rome; dies of cancer, Houston, 23 July.
>
> 1990 *The King,* a novel, posthumously published. (143)

By the decade's end, Roe says, "people were accustomed to Barthelme's shameless irreverence for short story form: his absences, his arias, his fiction's chameleon poses." But some still found his double-mindedness and messiness hard to take. "For instance, colleague Raymond Carver, once suspicious of Barthelme's motives, tried to make peace by honoring 'Basil from Her Garden' in *Best American Short Stories, 1986.* When Barthelme subsequently dissected this particular fiction and scattered it through *Paradise,* Carver felt betrayed." He had accepted the piece not as a partial novel but as short fiction. Barthelme tried to assure him that it was, and that he had no idea the story would be part of *Paradise.* The fact that it did end up in *Paradise,* sundered and rewritten in spots, can help explain his drive-by method of invention: "Basil" was autonomous—he had no thought of expanding it into a novel, evolving a novel out of it. Roe says: "Neither, of course, could Barthelme have imagined his own life when he wrote Damon Runyon parodies for his high school newspaper or hung shows in a Houston gallery or trailed his gods to New York City. In life, as in fiction, he trafficked in possibility" (86).

This calls to mind a crucial line in "The Leap": "I am cheered by the wine of possibility and the growing popularity of light" (*60 Stories* 379).

To "Basil from her Garden," Barthelme added a *ménage à quatre:* three attractive women moving in for eight months with 53-year-old Barthelme-like architect Simon. "Basil" is a dialogue between interrogator Q and respondent A. The two can be presumed separate in "Basil" but not in *Paradise.* Here, Simon is clearly identified as the respondent and at the end must be the interrogator as well.

Reviews of the novel were mixed, but Jolley in her *New York Times Book Review* piece entitled "Is Simon in Hog Heaven?" calls it "a revelation of a known and existing world that is fresh because the approach is unique. The writer offers an energetic prose controlled at all times by a powerful restraint. It is a very funny novel . . . also a sad book. Its form is dramatic; the drama is built up in fragments of conversation." She ends, saying that *Paradise,* "made up of the collision of brilliant moments, cannot be summed up. It is a picture of human needs and wishes and fantasies. Is Simon in hog heaven?"

Then comes her crucial question: "It is a criticism without judgment on contemporary American life. Is it just America? In addition to being funny and deeply moving, *Paradise* is a disturbing book because it is a fantasy of freedom in a world where there is no freedom. Is this just America?" (7).

THE TRUTH ABOUT HOG HEAVEN

The plot is straightforward, advancing in short chapters that can be dialogue, narrative, or question and answer. Simon, having left his wife, has relocated to New York and taken a large apartment. He meets the three women performing in a Lexington Avenue bar—"In white lingerie, hand on hip, the three of them, chatting with patrons, they'd just finished the show the bartender told him, fashion show every Friday, next week, nightgowns" (*Paradise* 12–13)—and offers to let them stay temporarily at his place. In the eight months that go by, the relationship between the four develops as far as Simon will allow and begins to disintegrate. In the process of the domestic matters of housekeeping and lovemaking, verbal collages—some highly condensed—define the nature of age difference: "*Simon you are twice as old as we are*" (63). But this disparity is not physical, even though Simon "lost nine pounds (a great blessing) during the eight months they lived in the apartment." (132); it's mind and spirit. Between Simon and the women—whose sum could be one Barthelme Snow White—the chasm is too great to leap.

Still, these four under one roof are altogether likable. The women live mostly in the immediate present, Simon mostly in the past.

He appears to be prominent in his field, acknowledged as such in *Progressive Architecture* (38*).* "He himself had settled for being a competent, sometimes inventive architect with a tragic sense of brick. Brick was his favorite material as the fortress was the architectural metaphor that he had, more and more, to resist. To force himself into freshness, he thought about bamboo" (58). One good thing about being 53, "you could enjoy the turning of a wheel. He feels every additional day a great boon." It comes as no surprise to discover that Barthelme expresses something very much like this in the Brans interview.

"When Simon wonders what kind of animal he is, he identifies with the giraffe. An improbable design, a weird ensemble overall, no special reputation for wisdom, an uncle-figure at best. Neglected by the auto industry: no Ford Giraffes on the highways. Simon too has a long neck. . ." (71).

New York gives him the facelessness he likes. "Simon enjoyed life as a ghost, one of the rewards of living in the great city. So many units rushing to and fro that nobody noticed anything much or had time to remark on strangers in the house, in the neighborhood." (119)

As soon as he realizes the long-range implications of taking them in, he considers his next step: "Send the women away. They're too good for you. Also, not good for you. Are you King Solomon? Your kingdom a scant two hundred fifty-nine thousand, two hundred square inches. Annual tearfall, three and one-quarter inches." He cautions himself: "You feedeth among the lilies, Simon. There are garter snakes among the lilies, Simon, garter belts too. Your garden is over-cultivated, it needs weeds. . . ."

As to what he thinks he's doing, "Simon had to admit that he *did not know* what he was doing. He was, he supposed, listening. These women were taciturn as cowboys, spoke only to the immediate question, probably did not know in which century the Second World War had taken place" (59). He surmises that they "derived their own politics from a K-Mart of sources, Thomas Aquinas marching shoulder-to-shoulder with Simone de Beauvoir and the weatherbeaten troopers of *Sixty Minutes*. They were often left and right during the same conversation, sometimes the same sentence" (132–33).

Not only does he listen, he constantly compares them: "Dore is brusque upon awakening, Anne cheerful as a zinnia. Veronica frequently comes to the breakfast table . . . pale with despair, then is overtaken with great gusts of enthusiasm, for *Lohengrin* or oyster mushrooms or Pierre Trudeau." Simon has actually met the popular Canadian Prime Minister at a conference in Ottawa, which "earns him about a crayon's worth of credit with his guests."

The women have a disabling effect on his senses. "They're so lovely that his head whips around when one of them enters the room, exactly in the way one notices a strange woman in a crowd and can't avoid, can't physically avoid, loud and outrageous staring" (42). Comparisons continue: "Dore is relatively tall, Anne not so tall (but they are all tall), Veronica again the middle term. Breasts waver and dip and sway from side to side under t-shirts with messages so much of the moment that Simon doesn't understand a tenth of them: ALLY SHEEDY LIVES!" Who this person Ally Sheedy is, Simon hasn't a clue: "In what sense does she live, and why is the fact worthy of comment? They know, he doesn't" (43).

He tries to universalize: "Dore is *crusty,* Veronica is *volatile,* Anne is *a worrier.* The generalizations are banal but comforting, like others he's been faithful to over many years, architecture is *frozen music* and art is *a source of life* (42–43). Later on, he notices that "Dore knows one trick which may one day place her among the world's managers, how to walk. . . . Veronica dawdles and Anne lurches, although at moments of confusion all lurch, banging into each other as if blindfolded. Simon shambles" (83).

And larger concerns loom: "What if they all lived happily ever after together? An unlikely prospect. What was there in his brain that forbade such felicity? *Too much,* his brain said, but the brain was a fair-to-middling brain at best. . . (100). "Someone would get pregnant, everyone would get pregnant. At seventy he'd be dealing with Pampers and new teeth. The new children would be named Susannah, Clarice, and Buck. He'd stroll out on the lawn, in the twilight, and throw the football at Buck" (101).

Or without children: "And what if we grow old together, just the four of us? The loving quartet?" (195). And the question for which he really has no stomach: "What kind of old ladies will these old ladies be?" (195). He sees himself as "a way station, a bed-and-breakfast, a youth hostel, a staging area, a C-141 with the jumpers of the 82nd Airborne lined up at the door."

Next, he's worrying about what will become of them:

> There was no place in the world for these women whom he
> loved, no good place. They could join the underemployed half-

crazed demi-poor, or they could be wives, those were the choices.
The universities offered another path but one they were not
likely to take. The universities were something Simon believed in
(of course! he was a beneficiary) but there was among the women
an animus toward the process that would probably never be
overcome, not only impatience but a real loathing, whose source he
did not really understand. Veronica told him that she had flunked
Freshman English 1303 three times. "How in the world did you do
that?" he asked. "Comma splices," she said. "Also, every time I
wrote down something I thought, the small-section teacher said
that it was banal. It probably was banal." Simon found what the
women had to say anything but banal, instead edged and
immediate. (168–69)

Veronica, for one, does not see him as a father figure. "'You're more like
a guy who's stayed out in the rain too long,'" she tells him and he asks himself,
"Does this translate into *experienced, tried-and-true, well-tempered*? Or *pulpy,
hanging-in-thin-strips*?" She says, "'I mean worn, but with a certain character'"
(112).

Of the three women, Simon mistreats the one most vulnerable, Anne. It
begins when they're making a salad, with Anne's unsophisticated response to
Simon's comment, "'Anyone who sees *Parsifal* twice is a blithering idiot.'" She
says, "You mean the movie."

For once, Simon's truly at a loss for words: "In any form. Land, sea, or in
the air."

And Anne says, with complete sincerity, "'Well I won't take you. You
have my word'" (22).

The word *dumb* has terrible power. He uses it on her when they're in bed.
She makes a harmless statement, and he says, "'The dumbest possible way to look
at it.'" She says, "'Well screw you'" (55). Soon after this, he's musing over the
fact that she "looks beautiful, her long dark hair done up in a ponytail. Her ARM
THE UNEMPLOYED t-shirt" (56).

Dore scolds Simon for being condescending to Anne, for putting her down
because she'd never heard of the Marshall Plan. He defends himself.

"It was a big deal, historically."

"Simon you are twice as old as we are."

"That does not absolve you of the necessity of knowing your own history."

"That's pompous. That's truly pompous. That's just what I'm talking about. And another thing."

"Oh Lord, what?"

"When you made that joke about George Gershwin and his lovely wife, Ira."

"Well?"

"Anne didn't know it was a joke. You can't make jokes that are based on people not knowing things. It's not fair. It's demeaning to women."

"Why to women?"

"Women don't pay that much attention to silly things like that. All that detail. (63)

Of course, Dore is right about the way Simon has treated Anne, but more important is why. When Anne becomes self-disparaging, it is he who shows sincerity:

"Look, dear friend," he says, "one would have to journey many days, cross mighty rivers and slog up and down towering mountains, cut through thick mato grossos with machetes in each hand, to find a more beautiful woman than your sweet self."

"Do you really think that?"

"Of course."

"Doesn't do me any good if I'm dumb, does it?"

"What makes you think you're dumb?"

"If I wasn't dumb I wouldn't be a professional model."

"Doesn't follow. Look at—." He gropes for the name of a model who is also amazingly intelligent but his knowledge of the field is inadequate. "Lauren Hutton," he says.

"She makes movies too."

"Tons of intelligence there," he says. "A glance convinces. Probably dreams three-dimensional chess. Q.E.D."

"You're very supportive, Simon."

"I love you guys."

"That's the first time you've said that."

"I slipped." (95)

160

It is Anne, of course, to whom Simon has been drawn from the beginning.
But only near the end is it out in the open:

> "Simon, I don't want to go," Anne says.
> "I don't want you to go."
> "But I have to."
> "I understand that. But you could be foolish and unwise."
> "You'd get tired of me."
> "No. The reverse, if anything. We could sit around and watch old movies on television. That's all I ask."
> "That's not true."
> "I ask you, formally, to stay. Will you stay?"
> "No."
> "Why not?"
> "It wouldn't work out."
> "We could enjoy it for a short time. Might be as much as two whole years."
> "You make it sound like a cancer situation. It wouldn't be fair to the others."
> "When is anything ever fair to the others?" (203)

The departure of the three women is like their arrival:

> "I got to go away now," Dore says. "I got to leave this place."
> "I gots to make mah mark in de whirl," says Veronica.
> "The prophet Zephaniah appeared to me in a dream," Anne says. "He said, Split! Split!"
> "Time boogies on," Dore says.
> They are gathered by the door with much duffel. Aspects of optimistic gloom.
> "Bye guys," Simon says.
> They lurch through the door. (206)

Simon's reaction is summed up in this statement: "I sleep very well, on balance" (207).

Veronica was correct in thinking he wanted them out (188), but not because he considers them "dumb bunnies" (187). Halfway into the novel, Barthelme sets up his "Hog Heaven" metaphor for the purpose, introduced in this passage:

Dressed women, half-dressed women, quarter-dressed women. Simon was, as the women repeatedly told him, existing in a male fantasy, in hog heaven. He saw nothing wrong with male fantasies (the Taj Mahal, the Chrysler Building) but denied that he was in hog heaven. Where did they get such expressions? A Southernism that he'd not heard in thirty years. (80)

After a confrontation with Veronica, who's complaining about men in general and Simon's "cheapo irony" in particular, telling him that she read that "Thirty-five percent of all American women aren't allowed to talk at dinner parties," (171) Simon reconsiders the truth about Hog Heaven:

In hog heaven the hogs wait in line for more heaven. No, not right, no waiting in line, it's unheavenly, unhogly. The celestial sty is quilted in kale, beloved of hogs. A male hog walks up to a female hog, says "Want to get something going?" She is repulsed by his language, says "Bro, unless you can phrase that better, you're chilly forever." No, that's not right, this is hog heaven, they fall into each other's trotters, nothing can be done wrong here, nothing wrong can be done. . . . (171–72)

So, if Hog Heaven is acceptable only for hogs, what of Paradise?

Simon thinks about Paradise. On the great throne, a naked young woman, her back to the viewer. Simon looks around for Onan, doesn't seem him. Onan didn't make it to Paradise? Seems unfair. Great deal of marble about, he notices, shades of rose and terra-cotta; Paradise seems to have been designed by Edward Durrell Stone.

Stone is a noted architect associated with the International Style.

Science had worked out a way to cremate human remains, reduce the ashes to the size of a bouillon cube, and fire the product into space in a rocket, solving the Forest Lawn dilemma. Simon had once done a sketch problem on tomb sculpture, for his sophomore Visual Awareness course. No more tomb sculpture.

And this is the thesis of the novel:

> Paradise unearned. It was, rather, a gift in this way theologically
> unsound. It was a state or condition visited upon him, like being in
> the Army. (186–87)

Paradise, like *Finnegans Wake*, begins where it ends, like a wheel, an endless loop in Simon's mind.

To O'Hara's question, "What's your greatest weakness as a writer?" Barthelme answers, "That I don't offer enough emotion. That's one of the things people come to fiction for, and they're not wrong. I mean emotion of the better class, hard to come by" (203). In 1988 Roe asks about lack of emotion, and he says, "A constant worry. I'm still worried. I tell my students that one of the things readers want, and deserve, is a certain amount of blood on the floor. I don't always produce it " (109).

Some readers would say that he makes amends in *Paradise*. He also reveals certain feelings about women.

Accompanying Jolley's review in the *Times* is a sidebar headed "We Can Always Marry More Men." It's an account of a visit made by Barthelme to Tempe for a reading of his works at the University of Arizona. He stopped in a drinking establishment crowded with well-dressed men and women, there for happy hour, as three young women, described as glamorous, paraded around the bar for the purpose of modeling lingerie. This was the starting point for *Paradise*, and later, in a telephone interview, Barthelme said, "It was apparently something that regularly happened. Very baroque." He went on to say, "I'm very fond of my women"—referring to the female characters of the novel. "First, I've met them in life. There's a lot of desperation. The choices are not so great for good women like these. There's not so much they can do. Remember, they say in the book: 'We can always marry some more men.' Then they realize that's not such a good idea" (Perlez 7).

The last lines of that interview express more pessimism than is found in the novel. *Paradise* would appear to close with some hope for the women and for

Simon, but Barthelme's statements cast a shadow. *Women like these*: the damning phrase is present, implicitly, haunting the pages of the novel; it's a hidden source of the tension, in tandem with a companion phrase: *men like Simon*. This hidden tension, then, is what makes *Paradise* the fine piece of work it is.

FACES IN A BAR MIRROR

Sam's Bar, Barthelme's collaboration with artist Seymour Chwast, contains 35 drawings of a New York City drinking establishment's regular weeknight clientele. The work is typical Chwast—woodcut or linoleum, inky, black-and-mauve.

Though there is the inescapable connection to the public house of H. C. Earwicker in the *Wake*, Sam's place shares more similarities with the old radio series Duffy's Tavern. Sam, like Duffy, is absent, and the customers enter to find themselves being served by Sam's second in command. "'The thing about Sam is,' they say, or 'There's only one Sam.' They talk about how all they're getting is low-fat love and what's the matter with me and what's the matter with the economy, the Japanese, the Japanese" (2)

The President and the Mayor are mentioned in passing, but Sam's customers are more inclined to discuss such questions as, "what about the condor? Not been a condor sighted in New York City for fifty years, the noxious gases from the Metropolitan Museum are to blame" (2).

Sam's name comes up now and then. Lester, a manufacturer, expresses more New York fear and loathing: "Let me give you one simple example: Sam's the type of guy you don't know what's going on behind that façade of warmth. It's real warmth, I'm not sayin' it's not real genuine warmth, only behind the warmth there are other things. The type of thing you and me might not think about" (6).

Some customers reveal their self-delusion, shallowness, empty lives. Calvin, a song stylist, says, "Music is my life but I can't play anything. Most of the people who can play something aren't fantastic. There's no point if you're not fantastic. Like Ray Charles or somebody. He was lucky 'cause he was blind. It gave him concentration" (16).

Twenty-eight of the 35 drawings are from the perspective of the barkeeper, that is, from across the bar. A third of the customers are turned toward someone, while two-thirds appear to be looking in a mirror, presumably behind the bar, either at themselves or at the person with whom they're conversing. In photographic terms, this is eye contact. It's especially effective in two of the more trenchant exchanges. In the first, Hope, a secretary, is questioning Adolf, a grounds maintenance man:

> Seen Sam?
> I seen his picture. In a magazine.
> What magazine?
> *People.*
> What'd he do?
> I don't know he was in the back of the picture. Standin' behind some guys.
> So for what did he have his picture in there?
> I dunno.
> You didn't read what it says under the picture?
> For what?
> It tells you what's in the picture. (54–55)

Barthelme has made his feelings known about people not reading. In 1971 he tells Klinkowitz: "This has something to do with television. . . . I invite you to notice that the new opium of the people is opium, or at least morphine. In a situation in which morphine contends with morpheme, the latter loses every time" (50).

In the second exchange at the bar, Tip is trying to come on to Rowena.

> The music business, Rowena, is not a business. It's a world. Good things happen to some people, and bad things happen to some people. Bad things happen to good people, and good things happen to bad people. But who are we to say who are the good people and who are the bad people? We *do* say who are the good people and who are the bad people, because we *know* who are the good people

and who are the bad people, but we do it with a proper humility. With an appropriate humility. Silently. Inside.

Rowena, eyes locked on her reflection, says, "We are the good people. I hope." She has class, this Rowena.

Tip, with cigar, dark glasses, plaid jacket, and polka-dot bow tie, is not Rowena's type, and she gets up to leave. "Time to go, time to go. I've got a terrible day tomorrow."

He gives this his last, best shot, watching Rowena as she walks out:

> Life, Rowena, is a song. By that I mean it's short, like a song. It's got an unhappy ending, like a song. It repeats itself, like a song. It can be loused up, like a song. You can go reggae or you can go heavy metal. You want fiddles I'll give you fiddles. You want synthesizer I'll give you synthesizer. You want to hear sandpaper, I got guys that can sandpaper your heart into little pieces So I ask you, is life not a song? Essentially? (61–65)

Sam's Bar ends with closing time, the clientele saying, "Maybe Sam'll be here tomorrow" (67).

TEACHER

Gass in his *Fiction and the Figures of Life* encloses in a parenthesis this sentence: "Barthelme is always instructing the reader" (101). His readers know this, that he's teaching us something about ourselves—flaws, better natures, options. In the eulogy, Barth says, "He was by all accounts a first-rate literary coach" (9).

He taught extensively in classrooms, in New York and Houston. He says in the 1981 O'Hara interview that teaching is rewarding "because the young writers talk about their concerns, about what's happening to them, that you learn from them [and] they learn from each other." At that time he was teaching a graduate workshop at City College of New York where "the writing students are fully the equals in seriousness and accomplishment of the other graduate students. Maybe writing can't be taught, but editing *can* be taught—prayer, fasting and self-mutilation. Notions of the lousy can be taught. Ethics" (189–90).

In the Brans interview the following year he has more to say about the classroom:

> I gave a student an assignment a couple of weeks ago. She was having problems because she was writing a certain kind of thing, and it was too tentative—it was too jokey—too whimsical. So I tried to deprive her of her humor. The assignment was to write something on the highest possible level of abstraction—say four pages—to see what she got. And I gave her a couple of things to read: Ashbery's *Three Poems*, Robert Wilson's *Letter to Queen Victoria*, and I forget the third. Not so that she would do a pastiche of these, but so that she would get some feeling for what direction the assignment was going in. She produced the most marvelous four pages—just marvelously inventive. It reminded me a little bit of Stein—at the top of her form. She was going along, reading it to the class—and at one point she reached down and tinkled a little bell. (Brans 134)

Brans mentions being "caught up in teaching." Asked about a connection between it and his writing he answers: "When you've spent all these years sitting by yourself in a room, you like to get out in society once in a while—that's the original impulse. And I'm very fond of the students."

Brans: did his writing ever benefit from his exchanges with students?

"In the sense that you meet new people and see what their concerns are, you see what they're worried about, you see what they're enthusiastic about—it's just like any social situation where you can get rather close to people over time— get to know them to some extent. It's refreshing, in other words, as opposed to staying home and sitting in my room spoiling paper."

Did he ever talk about his own work to them?

"Well, I talk sometimes about my own practices."

Did he ever show them how he did a story?

"No. Occasionally I'll read something that has some pedagogic value. For example, there's a story called 'Nothing'[19] [and if] somebody is stuck, I'll say, well, do me a piece that describes 'nothing.' Sometimes if I give that . . . when they're finished reading theirs . . . just to show how I dealt with it. . . ." One of his stories, "The Abduction from the Seraglio," did in fact come from a class assignment, "which was to do a version of Mozart's *Abduction from the Seraglio.* I had set it up in such a way that they had to make certain changes in the situation, so I got interested in these, and I did it myself. So there is some back and forth effect of teaching" (Brans 134–35).

Roe speaks of his "legacy to his students, who remember him affectionately as a munificent magus with one gene from Legree. Though he never sent his style armies to trample other writers' sacred land, he did expected untested troops to bleed their native talents." Roe says, "[R]eading one's feeble words aloud in class to the inexorable pacing of Barthelme's lizard cowboy boots could be murderous for a young writer unaccustomed to the master's scrutiny." But they readily accepted his criticism—comments such as "'Your sperm count is low,' 'Make her smarter,' or 'Try having her fall in love with the other guy'"— and marveled over Barthelme's ability to hear a story for the first time in the classroom and immediately know what it needed (Roe 88–89).

POST-CAMELOT

"A tender retelling of *Le Morte d'Arthur,*" the publisher prates on the back cover of the 1992 Penguin edition of *The King.* But there's not so much Malory here as pop myth, along with shreds of White's *Once and Future King,* Tennyson's *Idylls of the King,* and Wagner's *Parsifal,* an allusion to Dante, a mention of Milton, and the occasional nod to Shakespeare:

> "It must be true, then, what they say!"
> "What do they say?"

---

[19] "Nothing: A Preliminary Account," *60 Stories* 245–48.

"They say that when the mode of the music changes, the form
and shape of the state changes!"
"A most pernicious thought! It makes me ill!"
"Things yet to come will make us sadder still!" (*The King* 102)

As in earlier work, Barthelme is ornamenting legend with literature and
parody to instruct in certain fundamentals and qualities of narrative. In this novel,
King Arthur, some of the Knights of the Round Table, Guinevere and a few others
are holding forth during the darkest hours of World War II. At Dunkirk, the
British are in retreat, Luftwaffe planes are leveling London, Lord Haw-Haw is
broadcasting from Berlin—"'A fundamentally disagreeable voice,' said
Guinevere, 'stale cabbage'"—and Ezra Pound from Rome—"'He reminds me,'
said Sir Kay, 'of some old country squire, in Surrey somewhere, running on after
dinner to his poor bedraggled wife'" (7). And Churchill, all agree, "seems less
than competent" (55). Sir Kay—*cirque* is French for "circus"—is a composite of
all the King's men.

There are the usual jokes and intrigues, but the novel turns serious almost
right away. Guinevere says, "This is not my favorite among our wars. . . . Too
many competing interests. Nothing clear about it. Except that we are on God's
side, of course" (4). Mordred, who will go over to the Nazis before it's all over,
says of combat, "'It's theatre. . . . These great hulking heroes—Arthur, Launcelot,
Gawain, Gareth—come back to the castle all bloodied up, and people throw their
hats in the air'" (27).

What follows is the novel's argument, spoken by one who claims to be
preaching a new crusade:

> "The way I see it," said Walter the Penniless, "the old order is
> dead. Finished. We don't want the extraordinary, as represented by
> you gentlemen and your famous king, any longer. It is a time for
> the unexceptional, the untalented, the ordinary, the downright
> maladroit. Quite a large constituency. All genuine certified human
> beings, with hearts and souls and all the rest of it. You fellows,
> worshipful as you may be, are anachronisms. You know what
> happened when the Polish cavalry attacked the German tanks.

Why, the horsemen were smashed to flitters! A tank is nothing else but an expression of the will of the hundred workers who put it together. And they shall prevail!"

Launcelot and Sir Roger begin a discussion on food, hoping Walter will go away. But there's no stopping him.

> "We have plans for you, the warrior class," said Walter the Penniless. "Your functions, in the future, will be chiefly ornamental. Ushers, traffic wardens, overseers of car parks, doormen, elevator operators, that sort of thing. Little niches where you can do no harm. Not the life you've led heretofore but not, on the whole, a bad life."
> "This fellow seems a bit Red to me," said Sir Roger.
> "I've never met one," said Launcelot. "A Red."
> "Africa has a fair number of Reds, and they sound very much like this fellow."
> "I do know," said Launcelot, "that I'm damned tired of hearing about the Polish cavalry."
> "I get a sense that we're wasting our time," said Sir Roger. "That we should be out slaying dragons or something."
> "You don't bump into them all that often," Launcelot said. "Very few people in this world have actually slain a dragon. You will find a dozen vaunters in any great hall who claim to have done so, and the minstrels sing of many such triumphs, but what has actually been slain, in almost every case, is a lizard."
> "Lizard?"
> "Typically the Eyed or Jewelled Lizard, found in Spain, Italy, the south of France, and our own country, and which may attain a length of two feet. A largish lizard, but not a dragon." (37–39)

From there the dialogue goes into a joke about the only real dragons being Danish, but Barthelme has made his point, and does so several times more: Guinevere is "frivolous," for going a-Maying in "wartime, without a care in the world, when the whole world is embroiled in a most monstrous struggle" (43), King Arthur powerless, saying, "In the old days I'd have had her burnt. Just on the whisper" (59), and, finally, "far removed from the Grail of old" (77), a new Grail: "'A really horrible bomb. One more horrible and powerful and despicable than any bomb ever made before. Capable of unparalleled destruction and the most hideous effect on human life'" (76). The justification is familiar: "New problems demand new solutions" (77).

This exchange brings Barthelme's protest to its culmination:

> "And Grail-as-bomb . . . I don't like it."
> "Who likes it? But consider the logic. In former times bombing had some military purpose or other—taking out a railyard, smashing the enemy's factories, closing down the docks, that sort of thing. Today, not so. Today, bombing is meant to be a learning experience. For the bombed. Bombing is pedagogy. A citizen with a stick of white phosphorus on his roof begins to think quite seriously about how much longer he wants to continue the war."
> "There's that, I suppose."
> "There's a race on," said the Blue Knight, "to find the Grail. The other side is hard at it, you may be sure. Myself, I'm partial to cobalt. It's blue." (79)

The allusion to Dante, crucial to the novel, comes a few pages later.

> "I've quite lost my way," said Launcelot.
> "Lost in a dark wood," Sir Roger agreed. "With every possibility of misadventure."
> "The trees assume fearful shapes, because it is so dark. That one there resembles nothing so much as a flaming sword." (92).

This is the beginning of "Hell," Canto I:

> In the midway at this our mortal life,
> I found me in a gloomy wood, astray
> Gone from the path direct: and e'en to tell,
> It were no easy task, how savage wild
> That forest, how robust and rough its growth,
> Which to remember only, my dismay
> Renews, in bitterness not far from death. (Dante 3)

And in *The King*, Roger's subsequent observation is choric:

> "This forest simply teems with interesting iconography," said Roger. "There the trees limn a great chessboard, and the pieces moving by themselves, only they are the same color, silver, on both sides of the board" (*The King* 94).

In the 1981 Brans interview, Barthelme was saying, "I haven't seen a government I like yet. . . . I think we are governed by some very strange people. What can you say to this century with the two great wars and all the other wars and the concentration camps? Sorry century" (133).

King Arthur's decision reflects this: the bomb is out of the question. He would build a wall around England if he could (114), but no bomb.

> "We won't do it," he said. "I cannot allow it. It's not the way *we* wage war."
> "If we don't," said Sir Kay, "you may be sure that someone else will. Most likely the enemy."
> "That may be," said Arthur. "Still, we won't. The essence of our calling is right behavior, and this false Grail is not a knightly weapon. I have spoken."
> "Why, Arthur!" exclaimed Launcelot. "That's astonishing. Not doing a thing of this magnitude? I don't think there's been a king in the history of the world who's *not done something* on this scale."
> "It's a skill I've been working on for a long time," Arthur said. "I call it negative capability." (130)

The novel ends, with Launcelot sleeping under an apple tree, an observer speculating that he's "dreaming there is no war, no Table Round, no Arthur, no Launcelot." The other observer says no, he's dreaming of Guinevere, "wearing a gown wrought of gold bezants over white samite and carrying a bottle of fine wine, Pinot Grigio by the look of it" (158).

Here, then, an un-Postmodern irony: Barthelme taking the high ground.

TIME

When Brans interviewed Barthelme, he was 50. To her statement that he no longer seems as angry as he once did, he assents, telling her: "Gass objected[20] in *Fiction and the Figures of Life* to some lines in one of my earlier stories. The

---

[20] "A seriousness about his subject is sometimes wanting. When this obtains, the result is grim, and grimly overwhelming," writes Gass (103), in reaction to "Sandman," 1972.

male character asks the female character, 'Do you think this is a good life?' and she says, 'No.' And I think that got Bill upset at me, a bit, because he felt it was wrong to think that."

An admission follows: "And I wouldn't write those lines now, so I suspect he was right in being mad at me, to the extent he was mad."

She asks, "What has happened to make you think this is a good life?"

His answer: "Well, as you're in the process of leaving it you begin to cherish it more. That's true."

Brans says, "Don't say you're in the process of leaving it. I know when you were born."

"When you get to be fifty, you begin counting forward—you begin doing arithmetic," he says. In one of his *Great Days* stories, he tells her, "there is a quite clear statement to the effect that things become more exciting as there's less and less time. I think that's true."

She returns to the issue of his anger, saying that she observed a good deal of it in some of his earlier work.

"Probably true," he says.

She goes on: "I mentioned this to students, and they said, 'Oh, he's not angry. How can anybody so funny be angry? You're mistaken in seeing anger.'"

Barthelme says, "Joking very often conceals a lot of anger."

"Jokes are a kind of defense mechanism," she says.

"That's true. Gregory Bateson has a great line in which he says, 'Humor is the great alternative to psychosis.' It's true."

Later in the conversation he returns to the subject of his 50 years: "I like being this age. I don't want to be twenty again."

There is an ellipse in the interview transcript, followed by, "It's not that I'm uncomfortable being this age, I'm enjoying it very much."

Brans asks, "Just that the days are dwindling down to a precious few?"

"Yes, well, we're getting there," he answers.

To her next question, "What do you think the proper response to the world is, then?"

"Embracing it," replies Barthelme (131–32).

TICKETS

In the 6 March 1989 *New Yorker* Donald Barthelme's last short story appeared. It is "Tickets," an exquisite piece, full of those fractured-vertebrae sentences of his, many affectedly prim, and some showing the language speaking us.

Roe says, "If not a dazzling performance, 'Tickets' is one of those beautifully balanced meditations that returns pleasure with every reading," that "it confirms the even hand of the settled writer" (86–87).

The piece begins with this accretion of barnacles on the shipwreck:

> I have decided to form a new group and am now contemplating the membership, the prospective membership, of my new group. My decision was prompted by a situation that arose not long ago vis-à-vis the symphony. We say "the symphony" because there is only one symphony orchestra here, as opposed to other cities where there are several and one must distinguish among them. (32)

"Tickets" has a plot, a series of chess-like actions that cancel previous moves, subtracting them to attain a specific space. The narrator's wife, in possession of symphony tickets for a 9 March performance, is planning to attend with her friend Morton, when she receives an invitation from the artist Barbet to join him. "Barbet had extra tickets," the narrator says, "and wanted my wife to join his group and was gracious enough to enlarge his invitation to include my wife's friend, Morton." The narrator paraphrases what he has just said, as if confirming it to himself: "My wife could join his group, Barbet said, and took special pains to make clear that this invitation extended to Morton also." Morton, he adds, sometimes sings Hunding in *Die Walküre,* Méphistophélès in *La Damnation de Faust,* and Abul in *Der Barbier von Baghdad.*

The wife maneuvers to gain advantage:

> My wife responded, with characteristic warmth, with a counter-invitation, saying that she already had tickets for the ninth of March, including extra tickets, that Barbet was most welcome to join her group, the group of my wife and Morton and that the members of Barbet's group were also welcome to join my wife's group, the group consisting, at that moment, of herself and Morton.

Counting the narrator's proposed group, this raises the count to three.

So meticulous is he in reporting all this that his feelings for his wife are revealed. Roe sees it another way: "Fueled by the narrator's repressed jealousy, these simple gestures menace like rival nations' lying diplomacy" (87).

But what might instead be repressed in him isn't jealousy, is not in the least malevolent. What has happened is, the narrator has allowed himself to become odd man out in this relationship: "My wife had previously asked me, with the utmost cordiality, if I wished to go to the symphony with her on the ninth of March, despite being fully apprised of my view on the matter of going to the symphony."

He'd rather not. Attending a performance is something "that only the socially malformed would choose," he says, "there to sit pinned between two other people, albeit one of them one's own warm and sweet-smelling wife, for two hours or more, listening to music that may very well exist, in equally knowing and adroit performances, in one's own home, on records."

More defenses follow, and in the course of ensuing exchanges, we realize that this increasingly likable narrator is trying to change his status, to regain his wife, who is, it seems, a substantial part of his life. What is repressed can only be love, and if Morton comes with the territory, this is acceptable. Morton is her friend and no more, no threat whatsoever, judging by the early morning lovemaking that occurs between the narrator and his wife. As to Morton, the narrator says, "It is the case that Barbet actively dislikes Morton, whereas Morton is absolutely indifferent to Barbet." In a spectacular 192-word sentence the narrator tells us how "Morton acts upon Barbet like a rug that makes you ill" (34).

Morton, Barbet, the conductor Gilley (he pronounces it *Gil-lay*) who is sleeping with the new first-desk cellist Mellow—these are only rooks and pawns. "Tickets" is about the wife, about life and embracing the world.

Barthelme's joyful closing shares similarities with the endings of two classic films, Ingmar Bergman's *The Seventh Seal,* 1957, and Federico Fellini's *8½,* 1963, where the cast members join hands and dance on a semi-surreal horizon. All of Barthelme's characters could be in the group—the Angels, Florence Green, Airman Paul Klee, the Phantom of the Opera, Snow White and the Seven Little Men, and the three Snow Whites of *Paradise.*

This final artistic choice of Barthelme's is not jackdaw-like.

> My new group will contain my wife, that sugarplum, and her friend Morton and a Gypsy girl and a blind man and will take its ethos from the car wash. My new group will march along the boulevards shouting "Let's go! Let's go!" to inspirit their fellows, if there is a moment of quiet at the car wash someone will take up the cry "Let's go! Let's go!" and then others will take up the cry "Let's go! Let's go!," shouting "Let's go! Let's go!" over and over, as long as the car wash washes. (34)

---

*I think of the postmodern attitude as that of a man
who loves a very cultivated woman and knows
he cannot say to her, "I love you madly," because
he knows that she knows (and that she knows that he knows)
that these words have already been written by Barbara Cartland.
Still, there is a solution. He can say, "As Barbara Cartland
would have put it, I love you madly." At this point, having avoided false
innocence, having said clearly that it is no longer possible
to speak innocently, he will nevertheless have said what he wanted to say
to the woman: that he loves her, but loves her in an age of lost innocence.*

Umberto Eco
Postscript to The Name of the Rose

WORKS CITED IN THE CHAPTER

Barth, John. "Thinking Man's Minimalist: Honoring Barthelme." *The New York Times Book Review,* 3 September 1989: 9.

Barthelme, Donald. *The King.* New York: Penguin, 1992.

——. *Paradise.* New York: Penguin, 1987.

——. "Tickets." *The New Yorker.* 6 March 1989: 32–34.

Barthelme, Donald, and Seymour Chwast. *Sam's Bar.* Garden City: Doubleday, 1987.

Brans, Jo. "Embracing the World: An Interview with Donald Barthelme." *Southwest Review* 67, Spring 1982: 121–37.

Dante. *The Divine Comedy.* New York: Universal Classics, n.d.

Gass, William H. *Fiction and the Figures of Life.* Boston: David R. Godine, 1979.

Jolley, Elizabeth. "Is Simon in Hog Heaven?" *New York Times Book Review,* 26 October 1986: 7.

Klinkowitz, Jerome. "Donald Barthelme." *The New Fiction: Interviews with Innovative American Writers.* Ed. Joe David Bellamy. Urbana: U of Illinois P, 1974. 45–54.

McCaffery, Larry. "An Interview with Donald Barthelme." *Anything Can Happen: Interviews with Contemporary American Novelists.* Ed. Thomas LeClair and McCaffery. Urbana: U of Illinois P, 1983. 32–44.

O'Hara, J. D. "Donald Barthelme: The Art of Fiction LXVI." *Paris Review* 80 (1981). 181–210.

Patteson, Richard F., ed. *Critical Essays on Donald Barthelme.* New York: Macmillan, 1992.

Perlez, Jane. "'We Can Always Marry More Men.'" *The New York Times Book Review,* 26 October 1986: 7.

Roe, Barbara. *Donald Barthelme: A Study of the Short Fiction.* New York: Twayne, 1992.

SELECTED BIBLIOGRAPHY

Primary Sources

DONALD BARTHELME'S NOVELS

Snow White. New York: Atheneum, 1967.

The Dead Father. New York: Penguin, 1986.

Paradise. New York: Penguin, 1987.

The King. New York: Penguin, 1992.

SHORT FICTION COLLECTIONS

Come Back, Dr. Caligari. Boston: Little, Brown, 1964.

Unspeakable Practices, Unnatural Acts. New York: Farrar, 1968.

City Life. New York: Farrar, 1970.

Sadness. New York: Farrar, 1972.

Amateurs. New York: Farrar, 1976.

Great Days. New York: Farrar, 1979.

60 Stories. New York: Penguin, 1993.

Overnight to Many Distant Cities. New York: Putnam's, 1983.

40 Stories. New York: Penguin, 1989.

NON-FICTION COLLECTIONS

Guilty Pleasures. New York: Farrar, 1974.

Here in the Village. Northridge, CA: Lord John Press, 1978.

CHILDREN'S BOOK

The Slightly Irregular Fire Engine, or The Hithering Thithering Djinn. New York: Farrar, 1971.

ANTHOLOGY

Herzinger, Kim, ed. *The Teachings of Don B.: Satires, Parodies, Fables, Illustrated Stories, and Plays of Donald Barthelme*. New York: Turtle Bay Books, 1992.

DRAMATIC ADAPTATIONS

Great Days. Produced at American Place Theatre, New York, 8-26 June 1983.

Snow White. Rehearsed Reading. Produced at American Place Theatre, New York, 10 June 1976.

PICTURE-TEXT COLLABORATION

Sam's Bar: An American Landscape [with Seymour Chwast]. Garden City, NJ: Doubleday, 1987.

UNCOLLECTED SHORT STORIES

"Man's Face." *The New Yorker* 40, 30 May 1964: 29.

"Then." *Mother* 3 Nov.-Dec. 1964: 22–23.

"Blue Flower Problem." *Harvest* May 1967: 29.

"Philadelphia." *The New Yorker* 44, 30 Nov. 1968: 56–58.

"Newsletter." *The New Yorker* 11 July 1970: 23.

"Adventure." *Harper's Bazaar* Dec. 1970: 92–95.

"The Story Thus Far." *The New Yorker* 47, 1 May 1971: 42–45.

"Natural History." *Harper's* 243, Aug. 1971: 44–45.

182

"Edwards, Amelia." *The New Yorker* 48, 9 Sept. 1972: 34–36.

"Three." *Fiction* 1 (1972): 13.

"A Man." *The New Yorker* 48, 30 Dec. 1972: 26–27.

"The Inauguration." *Harper's* 246, Jan. 1973: 86–87.

"You Are Cordially Invited." *The New Yorker* 49, 23 July 1973: 33–34.

"The Bed." *Viva* Mar. 1974: 68–70.

"The Dassaud Prize." *The New Yorker* 51, 12 Jan. 1976: 26–29.

"Presents." *Penthouse* Dec. 1977: 107–109.

"Momma." *The New Yorker* 54, 2 Oct. 1978: 32–33.

"Basil from Her Garden." *The New Yorker* 61, 21 Oct. 1985: 36–39. Rptd. in Charters, Ann. *Major Writers of Short Fiction*. Boston: St. Martin's P, 1993. 101–07.

"Tickets." *The New Yorker* 65, 6 Mar. 1989: 32–34.

UNCOLLECTED ARTICLES AND REVIEWS

"A Note on Elia Kazan." University of Houston *Forum* 1 (Jan 1957): 19–22.

"Mr. Hunt's Wooly Alpaca." [Review of *Alpaca* by H. L. Hunt] *The Reporter* 22, 14 Apr 1960: 44–46.

"The Emerging Figure." University of Houston *Forum* 3 (Summer 1961): 23–24.

"The Case of the Vanishing Product." *Harper's* 223, Oct 1961: 30–32.

"After Joyce." *Location* 1 (Summer 1964): 14–16.

"The Tired Terror of Graham Greene." [Review of *The Comedians* by Graham Greene], *Holiday* Apr. 1966: 146, 148–49.

"The Elegance is Under Control." [Review of *The Triumph* by John Kenneth Galbraith] *New York Times Book Review* 21 Apr 1968: 4–5.

"The Current Cinema: Parachutes in the Trees." *The New Yorker* 55, 17 Sept 1979: 132, 134–35.

"The Current Cinema: Dead Men Comin' Through." *The New Yorker* 55, 1 Oct 1979: 103–04.

"The Current Cinema: Three Festivals." *The New Yorker* 55, 8 Oct 1979: 164, 167–68.

"The Current Cinema: Peculiar Influences." *The New Yorker* 55, 15 Oct 1979: 182–83.

"Not-Knowing." *The Georgia Review* 39 (Fall 1985): 509–22. Rptd. in Charters, Ann. *Major Writers of Short Fiction*. Boston: St. Martin's P, 1993.

INTERVIEWS WITH DONALD BARTHELME

Baker, John F. "PW Interviews Donald Barthelme." *Publishers' Weekly*, 11 Nov 1974: 6–7.

Brans, Jo. "Donald Barthelme: Embracing the World." Southwest Review 67 (Spring 1982): 121–137. Rpt. *Listen to the Voices: Conversations with Contemporary Writers*. Dallas: Southern Methodist UP, 1988. 77–101.

Klinkowitz, Jerome. "An Interview with Donald Barthelme." *The New Fiction: Interviews with Innovative American Writers*. Ed. Joe David Bellamy. Urbana: U of Illinois P, 1974: 45–54.

McCaffery, Larry. "An Interview with Donald Barthelme." *Anything Can Happen: Interviews with Contemporary American Novelists*. Ed. Thomas LeClair and Larry McCaffery. Urbana: U of Illinois P, 1982.

O'Hara, J. D. "Donald Barthelme: The Art of Fiction LXVI." *Paris Review* 80 (1981): 180–210.

Roe, Barbara. Roe, Barbara. *Donald Barthelme: A Study of the Short Fiction*. New York: Twayne, 1992. 107–11.

Secondary Sources

BIBLIOGRAPHY

McCaffery, Larry. "Donald Barthelme, Robert Coover, William H. Gass: Three Checklists." *Bulletin of Bibliography* 31 (1974): 101-06.

Klinkowitz, Jerome, Asa Pieratt, and Robert Murray Davis. *Donald Barthelme: A Comprehensive Bibliography and Annotated Secondary Checklist*. Hamden, CT: Shoe String Press, 1977.

BOOKS ABOUT DONALD BARTHELME

Couturier, Maurice and Regis Durand. *Donald Barthelme*. London: Methuen, 1982.

Klinkowitz, Jerome. *Donald Barthelme: An Exhibition*. Durham: Duke U P, 1991.

Molesworth, Charles. *Donald Barthelme's Fiction: The Ironist Saved From Drowning*. Columbia, MO: University of Missouri Press, 1982.

Patteson, Richard F., ed. *Critical Essays on Donald Barthelme*. New York: G. K. Hall/Macmillan, 1992.

Roe, Barbara L. *Donald Barthelme: A Study of the Short Fiction*. New York: Twayne Publishers, 1992.

Stengel, Wayne. *The Shape of Art in the Short Stories of Donald Barthelme*. Baton Rouge: Louisiana State UP, 1985.

Trachtenberg, Stanley. *Understanding Donald Barthelme*. Columbia, South Carolina: U of South Carolina P, 1990.

Walton, Gary Philip. "Donald Barthelme: The Modernist Underpinnings of a Post-Modernist Fiction." Diss. George Washington U, 1991.

PERTINENT ARTICLES, REVIEWS, PARTS OF BOOKS

Achelles, Jochen. "Donald Barthelme's Aesthetic of Inversion: Caligari's Come-back as Caligari's Leave-Taking." *The Journal of Narrative Technique* 12 (Spring 1982): 120.

Barth, John. *The Friday Book: Essays and Other Nonfiction*. New York: Perigee Books, 1984.

——. *Further Fridays: Essays, Lectures, and Other Nonfiction 1984–94.* Boston: Little Brown, 1995.

——. "Thinking Man's Minimalist: Honoring Barthelme." *The New York Times Book Review,* 3 September 1989: 9.

Ditsky, John M. "'With Ingenuity and Hard Work, Distracted': The Narrative Style of Donald Barthelme." *Style* 9 (Summer 1975): 388–400.

Eco, Umberto. "Postmodernism, Irony, the Enjoyable." *Postscript to* The Name of the Rose. San Diego: Harcourt Brace Jovanovich, 1984.

Gass, William H. "The Leading Edge of the Trash Phenomenon." *Fiction and the Figures of Life.* New York: Knopf, 1970: 97–103.

Gillen, Francis. "Donald Barthelme's City: A Guide." *Twentieth Century Literature* 18 (1972): 37–44.

Hicks, Jack. "Metafiction and Donald Barthelme." *In the Singer's Temple: Prose Fictions of Barthelme, Gaines, Brautigan, Percy, Kesey and Kosinski.* Chapel Hill: University of North Carolina Press, 1981: 18–82.

Johnson, R. E., Jr. "Bees Barking in the Night: The End and the Beginning of Donald Barthelme's Narrative." *Boundary* 2, 5 (197): 71–92.

Klinkowitz, Jerome. "Donald Barthelme's Art of Collage." *The Practice of Fiction in America.* Ames: Iowa State UP, 1980. 106–113.

_____. *The Self-Apparent Word: Fiction as Language, Language a Fiction.* Carbondale: Southern Illinois UP, 1984. 14–15, 30–32, 71–75 and passim.

Leland, John. "Remarks Re-marked: Barthelme, What Curios of Signs! *Boundary* 2, 5 (Spring 1977): 795–811.

McCaffery, Larry. "Donald Barthelme: The Aesthetics of Trash." *The Metafictional Muse: The Works of Robert Coover, Donald Barthelme, and William H. Gass.* Pittsburgh: U of Pittsburgh P, 1982: 99–150.

McNally, Sally Allen. "'But Why Am I Troubling Myself About Cans?' Style, Reaction, and Lack of Reaction in Barthelme's *Snow White*.' *Language and Style* 8 (1975): 81–94.

Meisel, Perry. "Mapping Barthelme's 'Paraguay.'" *New York Literary Forum* 8–9 (1981), 129–138.

Newman, Charles. *The Post-Modern Aura: The Act of Fiction in an Age of Inflation*. Evanston: Northwestern U P, 1985.

Rother, James. "Parafiction: The Adjacent Universe of Barth, Barthelme, Pynchon, and Nabokov. *Boundary* 2, 5 (Fall 1976): 21–43.

Schmitz, Neil. "Donald Barthelme and the Emergence of Modern Satire." *Minnesota Review* Fall 1971: 109–18.

Stevick, Philip. *Alternative Pleasures: Postrealist Fiction and the Tradition*. Urbana: U of Illinois P, 1981. 19–26, 31–40, and passim.

Tanner, Tony. *City of Words: American fiction 1950–1970*. New York: Harper, 1971. 400–406.

Upton, Lee. "Failed Artists in Donald Barthelme's *Sixty Stories*. *Critique* 26 (Fall 1984): 11–17.

Wilde, Alan. "Barthelme Unfair to Kierkegaard." *Horizons of Assent: Modernism, Postmodernism, and the Ironic Imagination*. Baltimore: Johns Hopkins UP, 1981: 166–88. See also pp. 45–47, 149–151 and passim.

_____. "Barthelme in his garden." *Middle Grounds: Studies in Contemporary American Fiction*. Philadelphia: U of Pennsylvania P, 1987. 161–72; see also 34–39 and passim.

188

The Arts

Arnason, H. H. *History of Modern Art.* New York: Harry N. Abrams, 1986.

"The Current Cinema: The Earth as an Overturned Bowl." *New Yorker* 55, 10 Sept. 1979: 120.

Frank, Joseph. "Spatial Form in Modern Literature." *The Widening Gyre: Crisis and Mastery in Modern Literature.* New Brunswick: Rutgers UP, 1963: 3–62.

Handke, Peter. *Kaspar and Other Plays.* Tr. Michael Roloff. New York: Farrar, Straus and Giroux, 1969.

——. *The Left-Handed Woman.* Tr. Ralph Manheim. New York: Farrar, Straus and Giroux, 1978.

——. *The Ride Across Lake Constance and Other Plays.* Tr. Michael Roloff. New York: Farrar, Straus and Giroux, 1976.

——. *A Sorrow Beyond Dreams: A Life Story.* Tr. Ralph Manheim. New York: Farrar, Straus and Giroux, 1974.

Herzinger, Kim. "Introduction: On the New Fiction." *Mississippi Review* 40/41 (Winter, 1985) 18.

Jencks, Charles. *The Language of Post-Modern Architecture.* New York: Rizzoli, 1984: 124.

Kael, Pauline. "Trash, Art, and the Movies." *Going Steady* (Boston: Little, Brown, 1970). 85–129.

Leavitt, David. "New Voices and Old Values." *New York Times Book Review* May 12, 1985: 1.

Legg, Alicia, ed. *Sol LeWitt.* New York: Museum of Modern Art, 1978: 168.

Reinhardt, Ad. "Timeless in Asia." *Art News* 58 (Jan. 1960): 34–5.

Tuchman, Phyllis. "An Interview with Carl Andre." *Artform* 8 (June 1970) 55–61.

Venturi, Robert. *Complexity and Contradiction in Architecture*, 2nd ed. New York: Museum of Modern Art, 1977: 16.

——. *Iconography and Electronics upon a Generic Architecture: A View from the Drafting Room.* Cambridge, Mass.: MIT P, 1996.

STUDIES IN AMERICAN LITERATURE